... AND AMERICA ATTACKED

MONSTER OF TERRORISM IN 21ST CENTURY

... AND AMERICA ATTACKED

Monster of Terrorism in 21st Century

Edited by

GOVIND B. MISHRA

AKANSHA PUBLISHING HOUSE

NEW DELHI - 110 059 (INDIA)

AKANSHA PUBLISHING HOUSE
R-37-B, Vani Vihar, Uttam Nagar
New Delhi - 110 059
E-mail: ektabooks@yahoo.com

... And America Attacked

First Edition, 2002

ISBN 81-87606-14-2

PRINTED IN INDIA

Published by M.P. Misra for Akansha Publishing House, New Delhi - 110 059 and Printed at Mehra Offset Press, Delhi.

Contents

Contents

Preface

Beyond imagination, America was attacked on Sept. 11, 2001 when monumental towers of World Trade Center and America's Army Headquarters Pentagon were hit, collapsing the entire structure of former twin towers—killing thousands of people and destroying the property of billions of dollars. No doubt, this heinous and barbaric act is a blot on humanity and must be condemned. But remember 'what you sow so shall you reap.' It is America who gave birth and patronized the modern world terrorism. Now US is the victim of its own creations. The retaliatory counter-attacks are on. Remember! this should not take turn to Islam vs. Imperialism (or Christianity).

There is no commonly agreed definition of terrorism. The definitions vary depending upon which side of the ideological divide the problem is viewed from one man's terrorist may be another man's freedom fighter.

Terrorism is premediated, politically motivated violence perpetrated against non-combatant targets of sub-national groups of clandestine state agents. The use of terror in one form or the other has been there since the dawn of history. One of the earliest terrorist groups was Sicarii, a religious sect active in Palestine around 70 AD. Terrorism in modern times appeared with its bloody manifestations during French Revolution. In the late 19th century, radical nationalist groups like Irish, Macedonians, Serbs, and Armenians used terrorist methods in their struggle for autonomy or national independence. Internal terrorism is relatively a new phenomenon in world politics. State terrorism and revolutionary terrorism being the major categories.

Whatever may be the ingredients of terrorism, these acts ought be condemned valuing the human and humanity.

The present book is designed to bring an exhaustive analysis of the world terrorism in the aftermath of terrorist attacks on America.

Various crucial issues like anatomy of terrorism, terrorism as crime, a sight at global terrorism, patronising international terrorism, terrorism in historicity, revolutionary terrorism, managing terrorist organisations, high tech terrorist weapons, Anti-terrorist measures, experiments in combating terrorism, profile of Osama bin Laden and a dangerous future etc. are elaborately treated in the present book. So this cannot be taken as a book for pastime.

The information is gathered from various authoritative sources to make it a dependable reference work. The entire matter is judiciously selected and presented in most logical way. The sources of information are secondary—annotations, books, journals, abstracts, magazines, newspapers, reviews etc. Hence no claim of originality.

I express my profoundest gratitude to all the great scholars and experts whose learned opinions/writings are made use of besides their publishers and copyright holders. I am also thankful to my friends and colleagues who encouraged me and assisted me one or other while drafting the present venture.

I am also grateful to my mother and brother for their moral support. At home my wife Parvati and kids—Swati and Sudhanshu have provided me congenial atmosphere to execute and finalise the work. Hence my thanks to them.

Last but not the least, Mr. M.P. Misra of Akansha Publishing House, New, Delhi, deserve all appreciation for materializing my efforts.

—GBM

1

And America Attacked

"Good and evil rarely manifest themselves as clearly as they did on Tuesday the September 11, 2001. People who we don't know, massacred people who we do. And they did so with contemptuous glee," said an American newscaster in the aftermath of the unconsciouable September 11 suicide attack on the Pentagon and the World Trade Center.

The World Supremo, mightiest America was at last attacked. World leader—equipped with the peeling eyes of a hawk watching every activity of the nations—small and big—the world over aerially, super computers, dreaded war weapons, supersonic aircrafts, ballistic missiles fitted with nuclear warheads, star war program, riches economy, big boss, CIA & FBI, remote control of architecting nation-states—like all big talks proved pigmy before the mastermind of Osama bin Laden, the terror incarnation.

"The World Trade Center is a living symbol of man's dedication to world peace." When Minoru Yamasaki, the chief architect behind the construction of the WTC, made this statement, he could never have imagined that—terrorism—a word which is the very anti-thesis of all that peace stands for—would lay low the twin towers. Part of the world's largest commercial complex, and housing many business, government agencies and international trade organizations, the 110-storey rectangular twin towers (1WTC & 2WTC) were designed by Minoru Yamasaki.

The tragedy of a tragedy that it comes uninvited. Nobody in America had an inkling that September 11

American Airlines Flight 11: Crashed into North Tower of the World Trade Center

Boston to Los Angeles

Waleed M. Alshehri*	Wail Alshehri*	Mohammed Atta*	Abdul Alomari*	Satam Al Suqami
25	38	33	May be 38	25
NA	NA	United Arab Emirates	Saudi Arabia**	United Arab Emirates
Daytone Beach and Hollywood, Fla.	Hollywood, Fla., and Newton, Mass.	Venice, Coral Springs and Hollywood, Fla., and Hamburg, Germany	Vero Beach, Fla.	NA

United Airlines Flight 175: Crashed into the South Tower of the World Trade Center

Boston to Los Angeles

Marwan Al-Shehhi*	Fayez Ahmed	Mohaid Alshehri	Hamza Alghamdi	Ahmed Alghamdi
23	NA	NA	NA	NA
United Arab Emirates	NA	NA	NA	NA
Venice and Nokomis, Fla.	Delray Beach, Fla.	Delray Beach, Fla.	Delray Beach, Fla.	Vienna, Va., and Delray Beach, Fla.

American Airlines Flight 77: Crashed into the Pentagon

Washington, D.C. to Los Angeles

Khalid Al-Midhar	Majed Moqed	Nawaq Alhamzi	Salem Alhamzi	Hani Hanjour*
NA	NA	Na	NA	NA
NA	NA	NA	NA	Saudi Arabia**
San Diego and New York	NA	Fort Lee and Wayne, N.J.; San Diego	Fort Lee and Wayne, N.J.	Phoenix and San Diego

United Airlines Flight 93: Crashed in Rural Southwest Pennsylvania

Newark, N.J. to San Francisco

Ahmed Alhaznawi	Ahmed Alnami	Ziad Jarrahi*	Saeed Alghamdi
20	NA	NA	NA
NA	NA	Hamburg, Germany**	NA
Delray Beach, Fla.	Delray Beach, Fla.	NA	Delray Beach, Fla.

Note : The original spellings of the names may vary.
Source : Justice Department.
* Believe to be a pilot.
** According to FAA records.

would witness one of the most horrific onslaughts on humans and humanity. Thousands have lost their lives to this catastrophic attack authored by terrorists. Unpredictable, of course, are the ways of destiny. As mayhem accompanied a mass murder, a few managed to escape death and live to tell their tale.

Like a fantasy horror film of Hollywood, the monumental great towers of WTC and Headquarter of Superpower's Army—Pentagon were hit, which the American could not imagine. It's a slight miscalculation of the terrorists that White House has unbelievable escape.

No doubt, on account of human values and humanity, this act was and should be condemned. But one should not forget 'What you sow so shall you reap'. The Justice Department gives and account of the episode.

Bush's Threat for Retaliation

The United States threatened to deploy its "full wrath" against nations which nurture terrorism and laid plans to avenge September 11 deadly terror strikes. Facing huge public pressure for an immediate and overwhelming response to Tuesday's carnage in New York and at the Pentagon, President Bush pored over his options with advisors at the Camp David presidential retreat in Maryland.

Defense Secretary Donald Rumsfeld added that "the best defense against terrorism is an offense." "That is to say taking the battle to the terrorists and particularly to the countries across this globe that have been tolerating, facilitating, financing and making possible the activities of those terrorists." Asked whether that meant striking countries that harbor terrorists, he said on Fox News Sunday: "We have no choice."

Top officials, citing operational secrecy refused to offer further details of planned retaliation. Rumsfeld said Washington was examining bin Laden's involvement in

Tuesday's attacks on the World Trade Center and the Pentagon that killed thousands of people and said Washington would wage a long war across a broad front.

Who can the US Count on for Help?

American efforts to muster global support for military strikes against those behind the bloody attacks on its cities have met with a mixed response. Here is list of responses and reactions from countries, and key alliances of countries:

Australia

Prime Minister John Howard said that Australia would join any military action by the United States.

Britain

The US' closest ally has offered its full support, but Prime Minister Tony Blair has insisted that any retaliation "must and will be based on hard evidence." Currently British troops are fighting a fierce battle against Taliban.

Canada

Prime Minister Jean Chretien said: "When action will be decided to be taken, Canada will participate but in which form I don't know."

China

China said it was willing to join the global fight against terrorism, but analysts said Sino-US difference mean the two countries face grave difficulties agreeing on what action to take.

European Union

The EU has vowed to help the United States identify and "punish" those behind terrorist attacks in New York and Washington.

Egypt

Egyptian President Hosni Mubarak said that any anti-terrorist coalition to confront the attacks on the US must be placed under the auspices of the United Nations.

France

France has pre-attack jitters, with the defense ministry saying Paris was "weighting up options" but had not earmarked forces for a strike.

Germany

The German government was also cautious, saying it would decide next week whether and how to take part in any eventual US military action.

India

India, a rival of Pakistan and the Taliban, has offered all operational help, both military and intelligence in the event of a US military strike in the region.

Israel

Israel has affirmed its total support for the US, while Foreign Minister Shimon Peres has called for the creation of an international task force to combat terrorism.

NATO

In a move unprecedented in NATO's 52-year history, all 19 allies solemnly declared that Article Five of the North Atlantic Treaty would apply if it emerged that the attacks were masterminded abroad.

Palestinian Authority

Palestinian leader Yasser Arafat has called on Arab states to join the anti-terrorist coalition Washington is trying to assemble.

Pakistan

With its proximity to Afghanistan and key links with the Taliban, Pakistan's support for a strike on the country is vital. Its foreign minister said the military regime would offer "full support in combatting international terrorism." Any attack must be authorized by the UN.

Russia

Russian foreign minister Igor Ivanov said: "In the fight against terrorism, we cannot rule out the use of force."

Kofi Annan on the Tragic Episode

"The terrorists who attacked the US on 11 September aimed at one nation, but wounded an entire world. Rarely, if ever, has the world been as united as it was on that terrible day. It was a unity born of horror, of fear, of outrage, and of profound sympathy with the people of the US. It was a unity born also of the fact that the World Trade Center was home to men and women on every faith from more than 60 nations. This was truly an attack of all humanity, and all humanity has a stake in defeating the forces behind it. As the US decides what actions it will take in defence of its citizens, and as the world comes to terms with the global implications of this calamity, the unity of September 11 will be invoked, and it will be tested.

"I have expressed to President Bush and Mayor Giuliani and to New Yorkers at services in churches, synagogues and mosques the complete solidarity of the UN with the US and its people in their hour of grief. In less than 48 hours, the Security Council and the General Assembly joined me in condemning the attacks and voted to support actions taken against those responsible and the states who aid, support, or harbor them. Of this solidarity, let no one be in doubt. Nor should anyone question the worldwide resolve to fight this scourge for as long as is needed. Indeed,

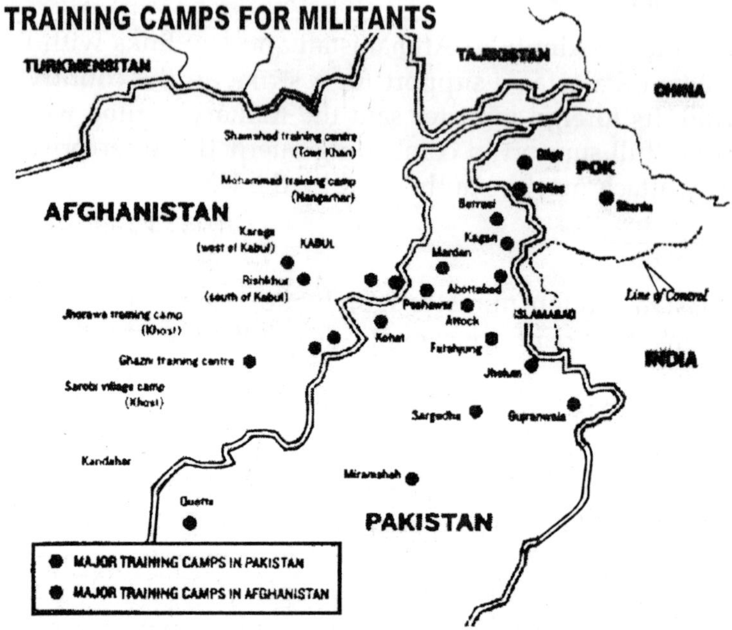

the most eloquent global answer so far to last weeks attacks has been the commitment of states from every faith and region to act firmly against terrorism.

"At a time like this, the world is defined not only by what it is for, but by what and who it is against. The UN and the international community must have the courage to recognize that just as there are common aims, there are common enemies. To defeat the, all nations of good will must join forces in a common effort encompassing every aspect of the open, free global system so wickedly exploited by the perpetrators of last week's atrocities.

"The UN is uniquely positioned to advance this effort. It provides the forum necessary for building a universal coalition, and can ensure global legitimacy for the long-term response to terrorism. UN conventions already provide a legal framework for many of the steps that must be taken to eradicate terrorism—including the extradition and prosecution of offenders and the suppression of money laundering. These conventions must be implemented in full. Essential to this response, however, is that it deepen and not fracture the global unity of September 11. While the world must recognize that there are enemies common to all societies, it must equally understand that they are not, they are never defined by religious or national descent. No people, no region and no religion should be condemned, assaulted or targeted because of the unspeakable acts of individuals. Terrorism today threatens every society, every people, and as the world takes action against its perpetrators, we have all been remained of the necessity of addressing the full range of conditions which permit the growth of this kind of hatred and depravity. We must confront violence, bigotry and hatred even more resolutely. The work of the UN must continue as we address the ills of our time—conflict, ignorance, poverty and disease. Doing so will not end every source of hatred and every act of violence. But if the world can show that it will carry on, that it will persevere in creating a stronger, more just, more benevolent and more genuine international community."

A Perfect War for the Elite Force

The Bush administration, confronted with a stealthy enemy in unforgiving terrain, is embarking on the biggest mobilization of the military's elite special operations units since the Vietnam War, experts say.

"This is the biggest test of special operations since Vietnam," said John Pike, director of Global Security org, a defense policy organization. "This mission isn't just about capturing one guy. It's a long campaign with thousands of combatants."

The role of special operations—which include the Green Berets, Navy SEALs and Air Commandos—in the new war on terrorism so far has been uncharacteristically high-profile, particularly because the military officially doesn't acknowledge the existence of some units, such as the counterterrorist Delta Force.

Military officials announced that special operations would play a key role in defeating Osama bin Laden and other terrorists. "These are people who operate in the shadows and we have to deal with them in the shadows," said US Defense Secretary Donald Rumsfeld.

A spokeswoman for the special operations command in Fort Bragg confirmed that the unit received a deployment order but would not say how many of its 46,000 active and reserve troops were being called into action.

In any given week, experts estimate that about 3,000 special operations soldiers are deployed on 150 missions in 70 different countries, conducting covert operations, training foreign soldiers and forging ties with various factions. The $4-billion annual budget for special operations represents less than 2 per cent of Defence Department spending.

Terrorizing the terrorists will be a top aim of the special operations forces, many of whom likely are working underground in Afghanistan and surrounding countries to destabilize and demoralize bin Laden's followers, outside experts have speculated. Locating and capturing bin Laden himself likely will fall to the prestigious Delta Force, which specializes in daring hostage rescues and kidnaping, Pike said.

Army Rangers would prove useful in attacking and destroying bin Laden's desert training camps and other targets, while Green Berets likely will provide assistance and training to local rebels, such as the Northern Alliance.

Air Force Air Commandos specialize in reconnaissance flights and will be key to evacuating other units. "This is the perfect war for special operations," said Carlos Moleda, a former navy SEAL who participated in the Noriega mission. "This is going to be more like a cat-and-mouse game. And special operations are great hunters."

Training of the command is legendary. Upward of 70 per cent of volunteers fail. Recruits learn to survive for weeks in hostile environments, eating bugs and rodents to survive. They scale oil rigs carrying 100 pounds of gear, parachute from 30,000 feet and learn to operate without sleep for up to a week.

Special forces

United States

•160th Aviation (Special Operations) Reg-120 troops; •Delta Force-800 men; •Green Beret-5,000 troops; •Rangers-1,800 men; •US Navy SEALs-250; •Numbers: 40,000, including airborne infantry regiments, elements of three of which are now in the region.

•*Best tactics:* Helicopter-borne assaults for quick strikes using massive firepower as cover;

•*Actions:* Kosovo 1999, Somalia 1993, Bosnia 1990s, Gulf War 1991, Panama 1989, Grenada 1983;

•Led by Special Operations Command, Macdil US Air Force Base, Tampa, Florida

War of Retaliation Started

At last Osama bin Laden, his terrorist organization Al-Qaida was held responsible for the dreaded attacks on the USA on September 11, 2001. After a thorough homework Bush Administration has started a full scale war against Osama bin Laden and his protege Taliban in Afghanistan from Sunday the 7th October, 2001 with the active participation of British army. And the fierce battle is on. Kabul is burning. A paupered nation is made scapegoat for the reasons of harbouring and patronizing Islamic fundamentalists.

This war against terrorism will be a long one. On the one side America is trying to establish it as a war against terrorism while Osama bin Laden and Taliban has declared it as 'War Against Islam' on the other. Thus, a hidden danger of polarization of Islamic Terrorism is there as the slogan of 'Jehad' is gaining momentum.

No doubt, to be religious is good for oneself and community as a whole. But we should remember, religion must have submissiveness and tolerance for other faiths. Let us see America's present retaliatory attack should not hurt the Muslim psyche. And a bitter Muslims vs. Christians or other Kafirs sort of problem could not concentrate.

2

A Sight at Global Terror

US dubs 29 groups as foreign terrorist organizations, the most deadly being the Al-Qaida group. It controls a vast network which can strike across continents.

It's not America Alone

Worldwide

•*Al-Qaida:* Established by Osama bin Laden in the late 1980s. Aims to establish a pan-Islamic Caliphate throughout the world by working with Islamic extremist groups. Has a worldwide reach. Financed by approximately $300 million that Bin Laden inherited from family.

Palestine

•*Abu Nidal Organization:* Split from PLO in 1974. Carried out terrorist attacks in 20 countries. Relocated to Iraq in December 1998. Operational presence in Lebanon and several Palestinian refugee camps. Operates over a wide area, including West Asia, Asia, and Europe. Considerable support from Iraq, Libya, and Syria (until 1987).

•*Hamas:* Formed in late 1987. Wants Islamic Palestinian state in place of Israel. Concentrated in Gaza Strip and West Bank. Receives funding from Palestinian expatriates, Iran, and benefactors in Saudi Arabia and other moderate Arab states.

•*Palestine Islamic Jehad:* Same goal as HAMAS, Receives financial aid from Iran and limited assistance from Syria.

• *Palestine Liberation Front:* Receives support mainly from Iraq. Has received support from Libya too.

• *Popular Front for the Liberation of Palestine:* Marxist-Leninist group founded in 1967 as a member of the PLO. Operates in Syria, Lebanon, Israel, and the Occupied Territories. Receives safe haven and some logistic assistance from Syria.

Lebanon

• *Hizbullah:* Radical Shia group, wants increasing political power here; opposed to Israel. Closely allied with and often directed by Iran. Operates in the Bekaa Valley, Beirut, and Lebanon. Has cells in Europe, Africa, South America, North America, and Asia. Receives substantial aid and training from Iran and Syria.

Philippines

• *Abu Sayyaf Group:* Smallest and most radical of Islamic separatist groups here. Some of its members have studied or worked in West Asia and developed ties with mujahideen in Afghanistan. Wants an independent Islamic state in some areas in southern Philippines.

Algeria

• *Salafi Group for Call and Combat (GSPC):* The most effective armed group here Algerian government has accused Iran and Sudan of supporting them.

Spain

• *Basque Fatherland and Liberty:* Aims to establish independent homeland based on Marxist principles in northern Spain. Operates in the Basque autonomous regions of Spain, southwestern France. Received training in Libya, Lebanon, and Nicaragua. Also appears to have ties to IRA.

Egypt

•*Al-Gama'a al-Islamiyya:* Egypt's largest militant group. Active since the late 1970s. Rifa'i Taha Musa a hard-line former member of the group, signed Osama bin Laden's 1998 fatwa calling for attacks against US civilians. Primary goal is to overthrow the Egyptian government and replace it with an Islamic state. Has a worldwide presence, including Sudan, UK, Afghanistan, Austria, and Yemen.

•*Al-Jehad:* Active since the late 1970s. Close partner of Al-Qaida. Goal same e as Al-Islamiyya. Wide network outside Egypt, including Yemen, Afghanistan, Pakistan, Sudan, Lebanon, and UK.

Kashmir

•*Harkat ul-Mujahideen:* Formerly known as the Harkat ul-Ansar. Based in Pakistan, operates primarily in Kashmir. Its leader, Fazlur Rehman Khalil, linked to bin Laden and signed his fatwa in 1998 calling for attacks on US and western interests. Operated terrorists training camps in Afghanistan. Linked to hijacking of IA plane to Kandahar. Has supporters in PoK, Pakistan, Kashmir. Includes Arab veterans of Afghan war. Cadres trained in Afghanistan, Pakistan, Collects donations from Saudi Arabia, other Gulf and Islamic states and Pakistanis and Kashmiris.

•*Jaish-e-Mohammed:* Islamist group in Pakistan, has rapidly expanded since it was formed in February. Aim is to unite Kashmir with Pakistan. Based in Peshawar and Muzaffarbad, but terrorist activities primarily in Kashmir. Maintains training camps in Afghanistan. Cadre and resources drawn from the Harkat ul-Jehad al-Islami and the Harkat ul-Mujahideen. Has close ties to Afghan Arabs and the Taliban. Bin Laden suspected of funding it. Recently USA has banned this group and sealed its bank accounts.

•*Lashkar-e-Taiba:* Armed wing of Pakistan-based Markaz-ud-Dawa-wal-Irshad. Formed in 1989. One of the three largest and best-trained groups fighting in Kashmir. Based in Muridke (near Lahore) and Muzaffarabad. Trains militants in PoK and Afghanistan. Gets donations from community in Persian Gulf and UK, Islamic NGOs, Pakistani and Kashmiri businessmen. Maintains ties to groups around the world, ranging from Philippines to West Asia and Chechnya.

Turkey

• *Kurdistan Worker's Party (PKK):* Aim to establish an independent Kurdish state in southeastern Turkey. Has received safe haven and aid from Syria, Iraq, and Iran.

Ireland

• *Irish Republican Army:* Formed in 1969 as clandestine armed wing of Sinn Fein, a political movement dedicated to removing British forces from Northern Ireland and unifying Ireland Area of operation: Northern Ireland, Irish Republic, Britain Europe. Training and arms from Libya and the PLO.

PIRA

- Provisional Irish Republican Army

Western Asia

- Abu Nidal Organization
- Armed Islamic Group
- Al-Gama'a al-Islamiyya
- HAMAS
- Hizbullah
- Jihad Group

Afghanistan/Pakistan

- Harkat-ul-Ansar

- Lashkar-e-Taiba
- Jaish-e-Mohammed
- Harkat-ul-Mujahideen

South East Asia

- Abu Sayyaf Group

3

Osama bin Laden: The Protagonist or Villain?

Osama bin Laden was born in 1957 in Saudi Arabia. His family has cordial relations with the Saudi King. Under the patronage of Royal family his family business of construction, ship transportation and communication flourished leaps and bound. On the instance of the King, Laden's family renovated the campus of holy Mecca-Madina. When Ayatollah Khomeni of Iran launched the Islamic Renaissance and termed it as *Islamic Revolution* in 1979, one Muslim student named Otebi also launched similar movement in Saudi Arabia. He captured the 'Kaba' revealing the ill deeds of Saudi King. Since, Islamic troops could not enter the Kaba, on the instance of the King, the troops of France and Belgium have had an operation in Kaba in which Otebi was killed. Laden was deeply impressed by Otebi but he did not revolt against the royal family at that time. He went to Afghanistan in 1983-84 as a messenger of Royal family, where Afghans were in battle against the USSR. Saudi Arab heavily supported to the Afghans.

During the same period Laden went to Sudan where he undertook the road construction and other logistics works. Here Afghanistan was trapped in civil strife for power capture. Laden drafted the strategy. In 1994, Taliban came into existence. In 1996, Taliban captured Kabul. Laden was the master mind of whole struggle. He became HERO of Taliban. He spent millions of Dollars and became trustworthy of Pakistan. And Laden drafted the New

Islamic World and gave slogan of Islamic Renaissance. Laden founded the organization 'Al Qaida' and established a network of nearly two hundred small and big captive groups known by different names. Resources were in abundance with Laden. He was arranging more than two billion dollars per annum through smuggling weapons and narcotic drugs. He was supported by Islamic countries directly or indirectly. Afghanistan and Taliban government proved a paradise for the Islamic Jehadis. His relation with Afghanistan strengthened more when he married the daughter of Taliban Supreme Mulla Umar in 1999. He became champion of Jehadis the world over.

Osama Doctrine

- The instigation for jehad against the Jews and the Americans in order to liberate Al-Aksa Mosque and the Holy Ka'aba is considered a crime, then let history be a witness that I am a criminal.
- When it becomes apparent that would be impossible to repel these Americans without assaulting them, even if this involved killing of Muslims, this is permissible under Islam
- Now infidels walk everywhere on the land where Muhammad was born and where the Koran was revealed to him
- Muslims are angry. The Americans should expect reactions from the Muslim world that are proportionate to the injustice they inflict
- It would be a sin for Muslims not to try to possess the weapons that would prevent the infidels form inflicting harm on Muslims
- The American army is going downhill in its morale. Its members are too cowardly and fearful to meet the young people of Islam face to face

- Whoever denies even a minor tenet of our religion commits the gravest sin in Islam
- Hostility toward America is a religious duty.

Osama bin Laden–A Violent History

"I'm fighting so I can die a martyr and go to heaven to meet God. Our fight now is against the Americans."

Elusive Saudi militant Osama bin Laden, mastermind in Tuesday's attacks, is widely regarded as the world's most dangerous man.

1990

The Gulf War and flow of overseas troops into West Asia fuel bin Laden's anger against the US.

1991

Saudis arrest him for slamming their decision to bring in US troops. Leaves for Sudan and begins setting up terrorist training camps.

1992

Claimed to have carried out attacks on US soldiers in Somalia.

1993

Believed by US officials to be behind first bomb attack on World Trade Center, in which six died and more than 1,000 were injured.

1995

Supports a failed plot to assassinate Egyptian President Mubarak in Ethiopia. Backs the bombing of military training facility in Riyadh. Five US service-men are killed.

1996

Sudan bows to US pressure and asks him to leave. Takes refuge in Afghanistan. Backs another bombing in Saudi Arabia that shatters an apartment complex housing US servicemen, killing at least 19.

August 1998

Believed to have planned the US embassy bombing in Kenya and Tanzania that killed 224 people, including 12 Americans.

2000

Officials believe the attack on *USS Cole* in Yemen that killed 17 US soldiers had the markings of a bin Laden operation.

Sept 11 2001

US confirms bin Laden and his Al-Qauida group are the leading suspects in attacks on New York, the Pentagon.

Bin Laden's Terror Network

Osama bin Laden has funded Islamic terrorism and militant groups from Algeria to Tajikistan. Much of this shadowy world is a mystery, but some of his activities have been more conspicuous:

1. Sudan: Expelled in 1996 under US pressure. May still own numerous businesses there, including share of drug plant.

2. Afghanistan: Fought in US-backed war against Soviets in 1980 s; set up training camps and helps bankroll the Taliban.

3. Kenya and Tanzania: Clinton cited "convincing information" that bin Laden plotted the Aug. 7, 1998 bombings that killed 263 people.

4. Saudi Arabia: Birthplace—and source of a multi-million-dollar inheritance. Stripped of passport, has vowed to topple the ruling dynasty.

5. Pakistan: Led meeting of Islamic extremist groups in Peshawar in June. Decision made to "hit American interests."

6. Yemen: Father's homeland. Son formed alliances with tribal chiefs, set up training camps.

7. Somalia: Supplied troops to fight US forces in 1993. "We inflicted big losses on the Americans," he later boasted.

8. Egypt: Funded Egyptian extremists and is suspected of backing attempt on President Hosni Mubarak's life in 1995.

9. Britain: Allegedly financed London-based Algerian group suspected of numerous bombings in France.

4

Patronizing International Terrorism

September 11 terrorist attacks on America resulting in collapse of two world famous 110-storeyed towers of World Trade Center and Pentagon have added new dimension to the international terrorism.

International terrorism has almost come to stay as a permanent system. During late 1960s and throughout 1970s, perpetration of terroristic acts had been a frequent phenomenon. The data released by CIA revealed that the number of people killed as a sequel to terrorist acts in various countries was 29 in 1969, 145 in 1973, 315 in 1974, 402 in 1976, 432 in 1978 and 581 in 1979. According to a study published by the *New York Times* in June 1980, the terrorist acts were committed in 58 countries in 1979.

The West European countries have the highest statistics of these terroristic acts. Of the terroristic incidents that occurred from 1968 to 1979, explosive bombing accounted for 47.6 per cent incendiary bombing 13.7 per cent, assassinations 7.4 per cent, letter bomb 5.5 per cent and armed attack 5.5 per cent. According to Yonah Alexander, Director of the Institute for studies in International Terrorism, there were 5,529 terrorist acts in the Western world. from 1970 to 1978.

The rapid acceleration of terroristic acts and the increasing number of victims pose a serious threat to world peace and under such a state of uncertainty no body can predict what may happen tomorrow.

Well-designed campaign has been launched in the West to "Soviet hand" in the perpetration of international terrorism. In order to camouflage its own imperial designs, the United States has usually described the national liberation movements as "terrorist". The former US Secretary of State, Alexander Haig once called the freedom struggle as "International terrorism".

Washington abets the perpetuation of international terrorism in various forms from direct involvement, through CIA, support to dictatorial regimes and promoting regional forces like Israel and South Africa. The role of CIA, as an instrument of US foreign policy, has been discussed in previous chapter. Here we deal with American support to dictatorial regimes and propping up of regional agents like Israel and South Africa for abetting international terrorism.

Support to Dictatorial Regimes

Though Washington calls itself as the cradle of democracy and swears by protecting the democratic regimes throughout the globe but it is a firm supporter of dictatorial regimes. No other region of the world has witnessed so many coups and putsches as Latin America where during the last 150 years there have been 550 instances of military take over. The region lacks political stability and absence of strong democratic traditions make most of the Latin American countries vulnerable to manipulation by Western imperial powers to serve their own interests. The United States resorts to all possible means, including subversion and open armed intervention, in its endeavors to thwart the victory of progressive revolutionary forces in Latin American countries. Washington also tries to consolidate and strengthen the positions of dictatorships by providing them generous financial and military aid.

Latin America occupies a special significance in American imperial designs. It renders wholehearted support to reactionary military dictatorships in Latin

American countries because it needs to assure the "stability" and security of its strategic rear and to safeguard US capital investments in those countries. It is also the Latin America that Washington has acquired the greatest "experiance" in organizing subversive activities and coups in propping up dictatorships.

The American strategic manouverability in Latin America for acquiring such experiences" dates back to the middle of 19th century. In 1857, a Californian filibuster named William Walker had overthrown Patricio Rivae, the lawful President of Nicaragua and seized power in that country. Washington installed a new ruler without delay. Since then the direct military intervention by the United States in Latin American countries has become a frequent phenomenon. That is what happened in 1903 in Panama where Washington imposed a humiliating treaty on the former for transferring to it the Cancal Zone. The United States after a six-year occupation (1928-33) of Nicaragua, installed its own puppet dictator A. Somoza. In 1954, Washington launched an armed intervention in Guatemala against the legitimate government of Jacobe Arbenz. There are numerous such instances where the United States has propped up reactionary military dictatorships having pre-American stance. The memories of the "secret war" waged by CIA against Chile and the US government's support of the reactionary regimes in Paraguay, Uruguay and El Salvador are still fresh in public mind. Forms of dictatorships by "corporate regimes" but the US policy of backing the most conservative reactionary forces in Latin America has remained unchanged.

American policy towards Latin American conservative reactionary dictatorships has been and continues to be same like it was an era of "gunboat diplomacy" or "good neighborly policy" or the period of "Alliance for Progress". The Nicaraguan dictator A. Somoza that "he may be a son of a bitch, but he is our son of a bitch", and President Carter in his message to Somoza in 1978, noted an improvement of the "human rights" situation in Nicaragua.

During the 1970s, Washington's support of rightist reactionary dictatorships constituted an integral part of the United States' Latin American policy. The reformist slogans of the "Alliance for Progress" period were gradually abandoned. The failure of the policy of reforms from above in the struggle against the revolutionary movement on the continent, the inability of "representative democracies" to ensure stability of capitalism in Latin America which the United States desired, the emergence in the region after 1968 of a number of military regimes with a progressive orientation (Peru and Panama) and lastly, the coming to power in Chile of the Popular Unity government thought democratic elections—all of these developments prompted Washington to peace its stakes on the reactionary military dictators as the only force capable of protecting its interests.

In 1971, United States stepped up its military aid to Latin American countries. Within a year the aid doubled to $ 150 million and by 1976 it reached to $ 200 million. This flow of substantial military aid was directed to rightist reactionary military dictatorships of Latin American countries who could play American role by proxy in the region. Washington had assumed the role of militarising the Latin American countries as its protege. The value of arms purchased by these countries rose from $ 148 million in 1970 to $ 531 million in 1974.

The advent of the Carter Administration in 1977 in Washington was hailed as "ushering in an era of human rights". From the mid-1970s, US campaign in defence of human rights assumed priority in its relations with reactionary Latin American regimes. But this was more of a mask to cover up American failures. The plank of human rights campaign which Washington had launched at a global scale was in fact a propaganda war against socialist countries. American strategy was to denigrate the Socialist countries on the pretext of so-called and imaginary violation of human rights and for that it could not very well avoid paying attention of flagrant violation of human rights by reactionary dictatorships in Latin America.

Another immediate reason prompting hawks in White House to wear the mask of "human rights" was the wide disclosure of American interference in the internal affairs of Latin American countries. Chile, first of all, of US actions in helping establish reactionary fascist regimes in the region, which put Washington in an unpalatable situation. The American image of being the cradle of democracy, adherence to human rights, well-being, respect for sovereignty and independence of all countries had been seriously eroded by it support of reactionary dictatorships and interference in the internal affair of Latin American countries. It was compelled to adopt the "policy of human rights" as a face-saving device.

The hypocritical "human rights" campaign get launched by the United States in Latin America was also prompted by another factor. By mid-1970s, the rightist military regimes in Latin America were faced with serious difficulties due to their inability to work for economic development and political stability, which imperialism required, and to coordinate their actions effectively with the interests of the United States. The "inflexibility" and "incompetence" of the reactionary Latin American regimes had been the subject of frequent criticism at numerous hearings in US Congressional committees. To some extent they were becoming inconvenient allies for the United States which time and again had to rescue them from the threat of revolutionary explosion and to help them survive since they could stay "afloat" with the help of US military and financial aid.

These were the major reasons in the light of which Washington under the guise of so called "human rights" suspended military and economic aid to the dictatorial regimes of Latin America. The termination of military aid and suspension of economic aid by the United States to Chile had least impact. First of all, the Chilean junta could obtain US arms for cash through Washington's trusted allies like Israel. In 1977, Us arms supplies to Chile amounted to $57 million which included A-37 and F-15 aircraft, firearms and tanks.

Direct intervention, massive arms supplies, destabilization of democratic and progressive regimes, unbridled role of CIA and support to reactionary dictatorial regimes are salient features of American foreign policy towards the Latin American countries. We have selected Nicaragua, El Salvador and Chile for the purpose of our study where Washington has played a havoc.

US Hegemony in Nicaragua

Nicaragua has witnessed constant US intervention in its domestic affairs. One of the important states in Central America, Nicaragua having an area of 1,48,000 sq. kilometers, has population of over 2.4 million. The country shares borders with Honduras and Costa Rica and sea coast touches the Pacific Ocean and Caribbean Sea. The ethnic division of Nicaragua is Metises-69 per cent, Whites-17 per cent. Blacks-9 per cent; and the remaining 5 per cent belong to Indian tribes.

Agriculture forms the mainstay of economy and bulk of population is engaged in it, which accounts for almost one-quarter of the gross national product. The new Revolutionary Government of National Reconstruction has undertaken various revolutionary measures to boost agricultural production.

Indian tribes are regarded as the original inhabitants of Nicaragua. The Azlecs and the Toltecs were one of the earlier settler who had come from Mexico during the 6th-

10th century. According to a legend, the country had been named after one of the chiefs of an Indian tribe – Nicaragua. Later when Spain established its colonial rule over the region they added the word "agua" and the country since then became known as Nicaragua.

The country of Nicaragua was disconverted in September 1502 and just within two decades of its discovery became subject to foreign invasion; in 1522 by Spain. By 1570, Nicaragua fell to Spanish colonialism and was included into Guatemala which was already under Spain. Nicarágua remained under Spanish colonial tutelage for about 300 years and this period was marked by various uprisings. In some cases the oppressed Nicaraguans had achieved temporary successes but the colonialist cruelly thwarted all liberation movements. However, undaunted Nicaraguan people continued their struggle to attain independence. The liberation movement gathered momentum with the passage of time. In the early nineteenth century, armed uprising flared up more vigorously and the Nicaraguans started demanding an independent republic. The liberation struggle of Nicaraguan people was closely akin to the liberation movement of other Latin American countries.

The sustained and protracted liberation struggle launched by Nicaraguan people resulted in a new, more popular uprising in 1821 which registered the retreat of Spanish colonialism. However, Spain resorted to various maneuvers to preserve its colonial hold over Nicaragua. In January 1822, the state was included by rebellious monarchist Agustin Iturbide in the Mexican Empire. But within a year, Nicaragua succeeded in regaining its independence and became a part of the Federal Republic of Central America. It was in April 1838 that Nicaragua became an independent republic.

It was during this period that Washington developed its hegemonistic designs over Nicaragua. The period witnessed a close Anglo-American colonial rivalry over Nicaragua. Britain had seized a part of Nicaraguan territory by the close of the 19th century. In 1841, UK established its protectorate forcefully over the Caribbean coast of Nicaragua and eight years later captured illegally one of the Nicaraguan islands. The United States forced the Clayton-Bulner Treaty which enabled it to obtain equal status with that of Britain throughout Central America. US policies in Latin America were distinguished by the staging of coups, provoking wars, fanning all sorts of conflicts and enmity between countries of the region with a view to weakening them and then establishing its domination over them.

The fluid politico-economic situation in the region was deemed by Washington as an opportune moment to perpetuate its hegemonistic designs there. There was a rapid flow of American capital in Latin American republics. In Nicaragua, US companies captured the fertile lands, organized plantations on them–growing bananas, coffee and other crops for export.

In 1855, one William Walker, with the help of American army, invaded Nicaragua and in 1856 he proclaimed himself as President of the State. Walker proceeding from the expansionist aims of Washington, intended to turn entire Central America into an appendage of the United States and a base of slave trade for the plantation owners in south of the USA. But the joint forces of Nicaragua and other Central American republics drove the American stooges away. William Walker was later shot by a firing squad in Honduras.

The United States lent its full support to the Conservatives in Nicaragua to suppress the national liberation movement. Because of American support, the conservatives remained saddled into power from 1867 to 1893. The vigorous pursuit of pro-American policy by the Conservatives had evoked considerable discontent among the broad sections of Nicaraguan society. IN 1893, one Jose Santos Zelaya, a liberal, assumed presidency. He carried out certain progressive reforms. But Zelays's policies could not serve the imperial designed of the United States. Consequently, the US despatched American marines to Nicaragua who hatched an antigovernment conspiracy and in 1909 overthrew President Jose Santos Zelaya and put one Juan Jose Estrada, a US stooge, as the new President, In 1911, even Estrada was replaced by a more docile puppet. Adolfo Diaz, a former employee of an American mining company. However, this was not the end of US Manoeuvred in Nicaragua.

In 1912, under the pretext of "protecting US citizens", Washington occupied Nicaragua. The country became almost a colony of American monopoles. During this period, Washington accounted for about 80 per cent of all foreign investments in the Nicaraguan economy. The Diaz Government followed pro-US policies. In august 1912, there occurred another uprising against Diaz Government and American domination but the ill-equipped rebel troops could not resist for long the numerically superior and well-equipped units of the US Marines and troops of puppet regime which received supplies from Washington.

USA seized this opportunity to dictate its own terms which formed manifestation in the form of the notorious Chamorro-Weitzel Treaty signed on February 9, 1913 between USA and Nicaragua. According to the Treaty, Washington acquired exclusive rights for the construction, servicing and maintenance of a maritime canal on the territory of Nicaragua. The US also got on lease for a 99-year period the Corn Islands in the Caribbean as well as the territory in the Fonseca Gulf on the Pacific coast for a naval base at a time and place determined by the United States. This Treaty granted US a perpetual right of control over the Nicaraguan coastline. The Chamorro-Weitzel Treaty was replaced by a new Treaty on August 5, 1914 which became known as Byran-Chamorro Treaty. Washington, by virtue of the new Treaty, practically retained all the privileges which further perpetuated US hegemony over Nicaragua.

Adolfo Diaz remained President of Nicaragua upto 1917 when he was replaced by General E. Chamorro who, was virtually an American stooge. There had been a continuous US intervention in Nicaragua's internal affairs between 1912 and 1925 and between 1927 and 1933.

In 1928, the US-inspired, so called elections brought General Anastasio Somoza Gaseva of the Liberal Party to power. He remained country's President from 1937 till his assassination in September 1956. The power in Nicaragua remained in the hands of Somoza family till 1979. The Somoza family patronized by United States ruled Nicaragua with brutal and repressive measures.

The Somoza family's dictatorial rule was challenged by the Sandinist National Liberation Front (SNLF) which was organized in 1961. The SNLF was named after Auguste Casesar Sandino, the great Nicaraguan patriot. The Somoza rule was almost shaken in October 1977 when SNLF organized a countrywide uprising against the American stooge. The policy of harsh reprisals and terror combined with maneuverers adhered to by Somoza in order to noose his political grip over the country resulted into an intensification of antigovernment actions and the growing isolation of the dictatorial regime both inside and outside the country.

Between 1977-78, the SNLF had organized itself as a force to reckon with posing a real threat to Somoza's dictatorial regime. The situation in Nicaragua witnessed a change during the course of the struggle launched by SNLF. The national leadership of the Front published a document. "The Programme of National Reconstruction" which laid emphasis that in order to quicken the process of the overthrow of Somoza tyranny, it was essential to form a provisional Democratic Government of National Reconstruction. It also called upon all political and social forces of Nicaragua to support SNLF.

By May 1979, the national leadership of SNLF launched the final operations for the liquidation of the Somoza's dictatorial regime. At the same time, the Front called for a general strike which starting on June 4, 1979 spread to the entire country. The Front was met with tremendous success. On June 17, 1979 the Provisional Democratic Government of National Reconstruction was established. The SNLF declared on June 26, 1979 that after the overthrow of the Somoza, a governing junta would be established to implement a policy of efficient democracy on the basis of a free expression of will and free organization of parties.

The SNLF had determined to liquidate the tyrannical dictatorial regime of Somoza. On July 20, 1979 the Front units supported by the whole Nicaraguan population smashed the pro-American dictatorship's National Guard. The Sandinist National Liberation Front assumed power on July 20, 1979. The triumph of the Sandinists served a severe blow to the US imperialism.

The massive US military to Somoza regime could not thwart the unabated emergence of SNLF. During 1973-78 the US military aid to Nicaragua amounted to $ 18,881,000 and US military sales during the same period to Nicaragua were $ 7,259,000. Besides the US also trained Somoza's army during 1970-75. The break up of trained personnel is: Combat Arms officers, 14, Command and General Staff Officers 10, Counter insurgency operations Officers 16, Urban counter-insurgency Officers 9, military police Officers 22, Military Intelligence Officers 12, etc.

There is no stronger weapon than that of the will of the people. The long struggle of the Nicaraguan people stand testimony to its. Though the Sandinists succeeded in liquidating the Somoza's tyrannical rule, the US maneuvered still posed a perennial threat. When President Reagan entered the portals of White House, the Nicaraguan revolution was already a *fait accompli.* During his election campaigns and after the assumption of power, President Reagan's anti-Nicaraguan stance has been discernible. Washington seems determined to do everything in its immense power to thwart the revolution from achieving its aims, especially with other national liberation movements threatening to undermine American hegemony in the region ever further.

Nicaraguan revolution is the fact of today and reality of tomorrow.

Guatemala

Guatemala is situated in the northern-east of Central America. Having an area of 108,889 sq. kilometers, its population is over 6,200,000. The country for long had been subject to Spanish colonial rule. It was in 1821 that it shed the colonial yoke of Spain and emerged as an independent nation following the breakup of the United Provinces of Central America in 1839. Guatemala has for long been subject to dictatorial rule.

The United States directly intervened in Guatemala affairs in early 1950s. In 1954, the Government of Jacobo Arbenz was overthrown by an army officer, Carlos Castilo Armas with the help of the United States. Washington spent several million dollars to overthrow the government of Arbenz.

The ostensible purpose of US intervention in overthrowing the Arbenz government was to protect the interests of United Fruit Company (UFC), a US multinational corporation operating there. Arbenz's land reforms programme included the nationalization of 234,000 acres owned by UFC. The Company was the largest US economic operation in Guatemala and its products accounted for a major share of Guatemala's foreign exchange.

The company was opposed to Arbenz Government and once its officials introduced 'a potential leader of the anti-Arbenz movement to two CIA representatives'. The Guatemala government offered compensation to the UFC which was denied by the latter. Washington failed to appreciate Guatemala Government's progressive policies. In October 1953, the US Assistant Secretary of the State charged that Guatemala's independence was being prejudiced by the international communist conspiracy'.

Soon after the Arbenz Government was overthrown by USA. the hawks in Washington tried to hide the truth by linking Arbenz Government with the Soviet Union. The then US Secretary of State John Foster Dulles said that 'events in Guatemala exposed the evil purpose of the Kremlin to destroy the inter-American system.' In his memoirs President Eisenhower wrote that Arbenz soon created a strong suspicion that he was merely a puppet manipulated by communists. These statements were purported to conceal the American motive in overthrowing the legitimate regime of Arbenz and justify the US hegemonitstic designs. This offers a stock example of how Washington could and can interfere in the internal affairs of progressive regimes.

Chile

Chile provides an extraordinary example of open US intervention in the internal affairs of other countries. Having an area of 756,945 sq. kms, Chile's population is over 11,100,000. Its population is predominantly Mestizo—mixed Spanish and Indian, and also includes German, Italian and other small foreign groups.

Chile had been subject to Spanish colonial rule for long time and attained its independence in 1810-1818 under the leadership of Bernardo O'Higgins. The country witnessed a long spell of alternating centralized and federal constitutions. Between 19\829-30, there erupted power struggle between Conservative and Liberal elements in which the conservatives emerged victorious. However, the Liberal group emerged powerful after the World War I. The beginning of 1930s witnessed the emergence of socialists and in 1932 the Chilean Socialist Party was founded. Dr. Salvador Allende, who later became President of Chile, played a key role in perpetuating the socialist movement in Chile.

United Sates always regarded Salvador Allende and his Socialist Party as a political threat to its strategic maneuvered in Chile. During the 1960s the major thrust of American foreign policy was to prevent Allende from assuming power. The US might failed to stem the tide of Allende's popularity who was elected as President of Chile in 1970. President Allende during his election campaign had promised internal reforms and nationalization of copper industry.

In December 1970, the Allende Government introduced a constitutional amendment providing for complete take over of the copper industry. The US had major investments in the Chilean copper industry. The other major US holdings were also nationalized. The largest of these was a $ 153 million investment that the International Telephone and Telegraph Company held in Chitelco, the telephone company of Chile. The other American holdings nationalized were Bethlehem Steel, various American banks and the Ralston Purina Company.

Most of the US companies nationalized by chile reconciled to the situation but ITT was extremely upset. The Allende government had started negotiations with ITT after having nationalized the Chitelo. But these negotiations were broken off in March 1972 following the disclosures that ITT had tried to influence Chile's internal affairs.

In 1970s, the ITT had resorted to an intensive lobbying in Washington to enlist official support for its anti-Chilean operations. The Corporation's president, harold Geneen met various US leaders including the then US Vice-President, Spiro Agnew. On July 16, 1970 Geneen contacted William Broe, the head of clandestine services for the Western Hemisphere division of the CIA, at a Washington hotel. Geneen offered Broe one million dollar to be used by the American government in Chile.

Washington virtually did all that it could, save overt military intervention, first to prevent Allende from coming to power then to foster his downfall. The US Administration had devised two distinct paths—Track I and Track II to prevent Allende coming to power. Track I involved foreign covert operation. An attempt was made to bribe members of the Chilean congress to vote against Allende. Frei, a potential rival to Allende was contacted through US embassy in Santiago. Frei himself could not become President and the one possibility was that legislature could elect Allessandri, who would then resign after having been elected, thus paving way for fresh elections that would return Frei. But this was a tedious and long way having remote chances of quick success. Thus Washington dropped Track I plan.

Consequently Track II plan was put into action. This involved direct contacts between the CIA and the Chilean military. Track II plan was given a practical shape on September 15, 1970 when President Nixon asked CIA to foment a military coup in Chile. However the Chilean army chief, Rane Schneider, disapproved CIA's proposal of a military coup. On October 22, 1970, CIA clandestinely passed machine guns and ammunition to anti-Allende group and Rene Schneider was killed by the group in a kidnapping effort.

Despite all these efforts, Allende was elected President on October 24, 1970 and Washington continued its covert political intervention in Chile. USA virtually stopped bilateral assistance. Aid grants fell from $ 5 million in 1969 to $ 1.5 million in 1971. American Exim bank credits which were $ 234 million in 1967 declined to mere $ 29 million in 1969 and were completely stopped in 1971. United States also opposed loans to Chile from international lending institutions. The Inter-American Development Bank which had granted credits worth $ 46 million in 1970 reduced it to two million dollar in 1971. The World Bank, under US pressure, gave no new loans to Chile between 1970 and 1973. Washington sold its copper stockpile to depressing international prices which lowered Chiles foreign exchange earnings.

The Role of CIA in Chile

Chile provides a classic example of the subversive operations launched by CIA in a single country. Commencing its subversive operation in 1958, CIA used economic sabotage, provided funds to opposition newspapers. parties and leaders, funded and directed anti-Allende labor unions in an endeavour to thwart Allende's efforts in becoming President of Chile. Consequent upon Allende's election, CIA used the similar techniques to create unstable conditions for the eventual coup. Both US administration and the CIA had been involved in Chilean politics since early 1950s. According to Michael Harrington, CIA's activities in 'Chile were viewed as a prototype, or laboratory experiment, to test the technique of heavy financial investment in efforts to discredit and bring down a government.

CIA actively participated during 1958 and 1964 presidential campaigns in which Salvador Allende contested and was defeated both the times. William Colby, former Director of the CIA, in a closed session testimony before the House Armed Services Committee, revealed that $ 3 million was given to the Christian Democratic Party in Chile in 1964 to oppose Allende in the national elections. Philip Agee, a former CIA operator, in his book *CIA Diary* writes how the money was funneled into Chile with the help of assistant manager, John M Hennery of the First National City Bank through the bank's Montevideo branch. Richard Helms, a former CIA director, in his testimony before the Foreign Relations Sub-Committee, testified that CIA provided substantial amount to Allende's opponents in 1964. It was also reported that CIA gave $ 5 million to Rev. Roger Vekemaus in 1963 to support anti-communist labor unions and to back Eduardo Fae.

William Colby's own testimonies revealed that $ 5 million was approved in 1969 to finance individuals who could be nurtured to keep the anti-Allende forces active and intact. After Allende's election in September 1970, CIA authorized another sum of $ 500,000 for anti allende operations. Subsequently in march 1973, the CIA provided $ 1.5 million to its chosen favorites for running the Chilean municipality elections.

Salvador Allende's election as President of Chile in September 1970 was a big set back for CIA as well as the entire US Administration. Washington pinned its hopes on CIA fore reversing the process. CIA was given a free hand. The agency started pouring in funds for anti-Allende operation by financing opposition newspapers and labor unions with an avowed aim of creating assistance to the *El Mercurio,* a conservative daily newspaper in Santiago for publishing anti-Allende news. It also paid $ 25,000 to help and individual to purchase a radio station.

CIA made extensive use of labor unions in chile for anti-Allende operations. In 1971, 5,000 women marched through Santiago streets protesting against food shortage and the ensuing visit of Cuban President Fidel Castro. The March was organized by the Christian Democratic and National parties of Chile who were pro-American. Although William Colby denied the involvement of CIA in this March but Ray Clive, former State Department Intelligence and Research Director, confessed that CIA did directly fund a number of anti-allende trade groups and labor unions.

In 1972, CIA financed the Confederation of Truck Owners' 26-day nationwide strike enabling them to pay strike benefits. In 1973, CIA paid direct subsidies to middle class shopkeepers, taxi drivers and truck drivers. Ray Clive observed that some of the money was intended for financial support of the small business and truckers in their resistance strike against the Allende government. CIA organized these strikes to cripple the already weakening Chilean economy.

All these efforts were directed against Allende government in Chile. On the one hand Washington sought to strangle Chile economically and its efforts in Track I and Track II plans having been miserably failed, the United States saw in reactionary military leadership of Chile a hope for revival of its strategic maneuvers against Allende. US increased its military aid to Chile substantially. Between 1950-1970, American military aid to Chile amounted to $ 8.5 million a year on an average but during 1970-73, the period of Allendel, it reached to $ 23 million a year.

Reactionary leadership in the Chilean armed forces were being carefully pressed by Washington to overthrow the Allende government. The higher cadres of the Chilean army having reactionary views, were frequently invited to Washington for briefing. After all, over 70 per cent of the higher officers of the Chilean army were graduates of US military academies and colleges, among them was also Augusto Pinochet. In 1972-73, Admiral E. Zumbalt, Chief of US naval operations, General E. Ryan, Chief of the Air force staff and other high ranking officers visited Chile to cultivate Chilean military leadership for serving US objectives. Washington made efforts to isolate the patriotic forces putting stakes on ungifted and venal Chilean officers.

Thus, the United States succeeded in alienating the reactionary officers of the army and navy on its side when the coup took place in September 1973. Aided and patronized by the CIA and Pentagon, the Chilean army became a butcher of their own people. The coup against the legitimate government of Salvador Allende was justified by Washington as a need "to consolidate democracy in the country. And it was the return of "Democracy" in Chile and protection of the American vital interests that made President Gerald Ford to declare the right of the United States to "destabilize" any Latin American government which did not serve US objectives in the region.

The reactionary regime of Chile headed by General Pinochet is an all out American puppet. After the coup, the official attitude of Washington towards Chile underwent a radical change. Whereas the democratically elected Allended government was deliberately refused not only aid but also loans, the reactionary regime of Pinochet received during 1974-76 over $ 2 billion in the form of aid, loans and credits from the United States. Repayment of the debts was also deferred.

Ostensibly, such liberal support was not provided by Washington to Chile for strengthening "democracy". The new military junta abrogated all progressive transformations carried out the Allende Government and began to denationalization of the Chilean economy on a vaster scale. Enterprises owned previously by foreign concerns, especially by the Americans were returned to their "owners". A model of "market economy" chalked out by American economists was introduced in Chile which again restored US multinationals their monopoly. The American therapy to the ailing Chilean economy failed to put the house in order. A year after the coup, industrial production in Chile registered a sharp decline with inflation rate reaching 400 per cent and the number of unemployed reaching half a million in a country having a population of eight million. According to *Financial Times* of London, during 1974, over 85 per cent of Chile on lived in conditions of extreme poverty.

What United Sates gained in Chile by overthrowing the legitimate government of Salvador Allende was its mere ambition of global hegemony. What the Chileans got in return is reactionary pro-US Pinochet regime, extreme poverty and repression.

The Case of El Salvador

El Salvador, another Latin American country, has been subject to US maneuvers and intervention. The country provides a live example of the operation of Monroe Doctrine. The Monroe Doctrine, as propounded by American President James Monroe in 1823, envisages that the *US would not view with tolerance the intrusion of any extra-continental power in the Western Hemisphere.* During the post-World War II period, the United States had taken unto itself the self-assumed onus of protecting the Latin American countries from the impending threat of "communism". The massive US aid to the reactionary military junta in El Salvador in recent years is the direct evidence of Washington's strategy of perpetuation its hegemonistic designs in countries wrought with political instability.

El Salvador is one of the densely populated countries of Central America. Following the attainment of independence in 1838, El Salvador has been frequently subject to political instability and repression. Bulk of the population is reeling under appalling poverty coupled with accumulation of wealth and power in the hands of few families.

The 1960s witnessed mild economic reforms but the political power almost remained in the hands of conservatives backed with reactionary military junta. During 1970s, the genuine grievances of the poor and landless were met with repression and terror. President Napoleon Durate's reactionary Junat regime had come in severe criticism both at home and abroad for resorting to repressive measures. The entire Salvadoran population whole-heartedly supported the progressive forces in the country.

The United States which has rendered substantial aid to the right-wing military junta with sophisticated weapons, felt panicky at latter's failure in containing rise of progressive anti-Junta forces in El Salvador. Washington temporarily suspended its military aid to El Salvador following the murder of four American church-women in mid-1980s. But in the wake of advancing resistance forces and their gaining strength, the US Administration authorized in January 1981 the emergency delivery of $ 5 million aid.

President Reagan soon after entering the White House felt military situation in El Salvador as grave and stepped up military aid with specific instructions to counter the leftist insurgency. By March 1981, thee were 45 non-combant US advisers in El Salvador to impart training to the local army and navy in counter-insurgency programs. US also agreed to provide $ 26 million to the already committed $ 10 million aid to help El Salvador to buy defence equipment, among other things, small arms, radars and surveillance equipment.

President Reagan's hypocritical approach to El Salvador has been widely nailed out. He justified offer of arms aid to help the forces that were supporting human rights in El Salvador. However, a former US ambassador to El Salvador, Robert White, while testifying before the Congressional sub-committee said that the insurgency in El Salvador was caused by social injustice and the chief killer of Salvadorans was the government security forces.

The reactionary Durate regime was solely baking on the US support. It is remarkable that small group of ill-equipped 6,000 strong anti junta guerilla forces have defeated 16,000 strong and US backed junta forces and have liberated more than one third of the country's 21,400 sq. km territory.

Washington is desperately trying to thwart guerillas from capturing power by hatching and putting into operation one plan after another. Reagan Administration is funneling more arms and economic aid into El Salvador on the plea that Durate regime is "making progress" in preserving human rights. Washington seems to have turned a deaf ear to the report of mass killings of unarmed civilians, women and children submitted by members of US Congress and Senate. Over 50 senators and congressmen and 400 US religious leaders have called for an immediate suspension of US military aid to the reactionary junta regime.

But Reagan administration does not care for the same advice. Not only more Us airforce pilots and special technical personnel were rushed to assist the Salvadoran miliary, but also President Reagan declared that the United States would do whatever necessary to save the Durate regime. Washington seems to be blind to the truth that but for a handful of tis stooges, almost entire population of El Salvador sympathizes with the struggle of guerilla forces.

The junta's mass extermination plan has already claimed 32,000 lives, compelling about 300,000 people to flee to other countries and an equal number of people have been displace. The people of El Salvador are living in a miserable plight. Half of the children die before the age of two due to malnutrition; five per cent of the people enjoy 40 per cent of nation's income; 50 per cent of the able-bodied are unemployed and 50 per cent of peasants are landless. It is in that poverty and misery stricken country that Washington is safeguarding human rights by supplying arms to the reactionary regime.

In order to cover its own hegemonistic designs, Washington has blamed the Soviet Union, Cuba and Nicaragua for supplying arms to the Salvadoran guerillas. The Nicaraguan foreign minister, Mignel d'Escoto openly challenged the United States to prove that his country was involved in El Salvador. The *New York Times* correspondent Raymond Rounea, who visited El Salvador, wrote in his account that none among the guerillas had ever gone to Cuba or Nicaragua for training and that the guerillas use the arms which they captured from the government troops.

Washington is not serious about the political solution of El Salvador. It is rather preparing for a direct military intervention on one pretext or the other. American indirect involvement is exposed by the Colombian Broadcasting Service's video taping of three US military personnel carrying M-16 automatic rifles, M-79 grenades and other combat equipment. The US hegemonislic maneuvers in the region are further substantiated through Washington's finalization of "Caribbean Basin Plan", altering of five US marine brigades and arming and training of an exile army of 6,000 in 20 training camps in cooperation with Honduras, Guatemala and Argentina. The finalization of the pact, with US blessings, among Costa Rica, El Salvador and Honduras and the Pact's declaration that the three states could seek "foreign military intervention to combat terrorism" is a living example of American imperial designs with far reaching implications for the entire Central America.

Washington has started attaching considerable importance to Latin America in recent years. Mrs. Jean Kirkpatrick, US Ambassador to the United Nations said recently that 'Central America is the most important place in the world for the US today'. Even the former Secretary of State Alexander Haig admitted that US policy makers believe in all sincerity that they have no alternative but to prevent forces hostile to the United States and the West from overthrowing a government on their doorstep.

5

A Dangerous Future

The Destructive Potential of Criminal Arsenals

Twenty years ago, the first debates about terrorist weapons and objective took form in the United States. Focusing on counterterrorist strategies, the Central Intelligence Agency and the Department of State, Defense, and Energy fought over bureaucratic leadership while authority within the Federal Bureau of Investigation (FBI) was divided internally between the Hoover-bureau model and the FBI Academy. The Academy led much of the intellectual debate, an exception to its previously less influential character. Overall, the FBI led the fight against domestic terrorism while the Cabinet Committee to Combat Terrorism working group became the interagency leader in coping with terrorism abroad. Among the members of the US counterterrorism community, there existed a tense atmosphere of fear when terrorist incidents occurred and boredom when they did not.

Given advances in technology and the increase availability of weapons of mass destruction, it is time to reassess terrorism. The geopolitics of global criminality have changed rapidly during the past two decades, granting tomorrow's criminals access to vast information bases and weaponry. Consequently, law enforcement has become an essential part of any comprehensive national security strategy. Enforcement agencies will face greater challenges as they attempt to understand and effectively confront the terrorism and organized crime of the future. Crime will be sophisticated and possibly subtle, and the United States must be prepared to cope with domestic terrorist attacks fare more severe than the World Trade Center bombing. With the world changing in ever more dangerous ways—and becoming ever more threatened by unconventional terrorist attacks—now is the time to think ahead.

Different Assessments

In a 1993 speech before a Departmental of Defense audience, Jenkins acknowledged that forecasting terrorism was largely speculative. Having offered this caution and noting the decline of superpower competition and the spread of anti-American sentiments, he then made a number of conservative predictions. There would be little technological change in terrorist tactics, he stated, although some might use more standoff weaponry and command-detonated bombs. Without fear of self-contradiction, Jenkins then suggested that terrorists may use nuclear, radiological, chemical, or biological weapons and computer viruses. But he claimed that even if terrorists were to use chemical attacks, they could design them to prevent mass casualties. Furthermore, terrorists have yet to attacks well-defended or truly high-tech targets, or attempt to penetrate computers of employ poisons or toxic chemicals. Jenkins concluded that terrorism overall will persist. He argued that Middle Easter terrorism will remain the greatest threat, that terrorist spill-over from guerrilla wars will continue but not lead to major crises, and that terrorist activities in Wester Europe will tape off. He predicted new sources of violence in the Balkans, the former Soviet Union, and Asia as well as new threats to the United States from narcotics traffickers, North Korean operatives, Islamic extremists, and issue-oriented extremist. Finally, Jenkis argued that while high-casualty character of terrorist operations would not change dramatically, and that mass destruction terrorism is highly unlikely.

Jenkins, moreover, does not adequately address several policy and operational problems. First, if, for example, terrorist do go high-tech, no government agency currently exists to cope with the repercussions of their attack. The physical and psychological costs of such a major high-tech offensive in the United States could prove overwhelming. In this context, it is important to note the tacit assumption that terrorists are incapable of seriously miscalculating the consequences of their attack. Second, many seasoned observers and federal law enforcement officials assume that an unstated agreement exists between the West and terrorist-sponsoring nations such as Iran and Syria. This understanding holds that state-sponsors will restrain terrorists from engaging in massive attacks, leaving their attacks as little more than annoyances. Yet this view fails to acknowledge that had the World Trade Center bombing been better designed, thousands could have died and the US financial community could have come to a grinding halt. Several of the terrorists captured were planning attacks of monumental proportions—Manhattan would have been severely damaged. Future security is increasingly threatened as terrorism becomes enmeshed in the fabric of global organized crime. The growing global interconnectivity of organized crime—with its vast resources and its ability to move money, share information, exploit and manipulate modem technology, and provide endless quantities of black market commodities—has forever changed the way terrorists do business. Terrorists have always sought leverage to penetrate international power and influence. A major change today is that otherwise small and insignificant terrorist groups can join with organized crime to exercise disproportionate leverage. We used to think that small groups could only execute small acts of violence. Because of the benefits accruing from these new criminal arrangements, however, this may no longer be the case. An essential question emerges as to whether terrorists are becoming transformed globally into organized criminals or are just using the funds generated by their own criminal activities to support their terrorist agendas.

Another troubling security issue that will face is the plethora of target choices available to terrorists, the most tempting of which may be infrastructural, such as the information superhighway. As information is the currency of the future, the potential exploitation of this target deserves priority consideration. Everything from currencies to stocks and bonds to corporate secrets are now stored in electronic formats. Never before has information been more accessible or susceptible to interception, contamination, or even complete deletion. Moreover, elements of the civilian, financial, intelligence, law enforcement, and military communities are becoming dependent on information transmitted electronically on the information superhighway for the daily conduct of their affairs. Information systems are vulnerable to both traditional physical threats (hard attacks) as well as to forms of soft attack, including jamming, "spoofing," hacking and over-loading electrical circuits. In 1988, for example, Rober Morris injected a malicious code dubbed "Worm" into the Internet, bringing the entire system to a complete standstill. The emerging information superhighway may take on new dimensions of vulnerability in the future. The horrifying prospect of infrastructural attacks by terrorists may cause law enforcement agencies to simply throw up their hands. Technological interconnections have become so integral to our lives as to be virtually invisible. Deliberately targeted attacks—for example, on the Public Switched Network or FedWire—could bring an industrialized society to a temporary, but lengthy, halt through the disruption of interlocking networks. A major power failure could interrupt the Internet and other computer networks, food supply chains sanitation and water system, fuel provision systems, and transportation systems.

Threat to the United States

The increasing aggressiveness and effectiveness of terrorist attacks became evident to the American public with the bombing of the World Trade Center on February 26, 1993. Until then, the FBI and local law enforcement had been complacent about the possibility of major acts of international terrorism occurring in the United States. Yet the bombing shocked the US government into recognizing that international terrorism is among the nation's most important law enforcement and national security challenges. Numerous challenges exist to contemporary US counterterrorist efforts. First, budget cuts, loss of expertise, and lack of focus have limited foreign counterterrorism—the first line of defense against international terrorism. International cooperation, an effective and necessary method of deterring terrorism, has all too often been treated as a minor political function in the Department of State. Second, local law enforcement units are poorly trained to detect and deter terrorism. Overreaction can lead to the violation of human rights and the alienation that leads to political violence. The Immigration and Naturalization Service (INS) is overwhelmed, under-trained, and unprepared to regulate legal immigration or to track illegal immigrants who enter the United States. The Federal Emergency Management Agency (FEMA), responsible for confronting the consequences of terrorist attacks, is incapable of rapid and effective response.

Although the United States was a target for international terrorist activities, including bombing and hostage-taking, throughout the 1980s, the American mainland was never directly threatened. Americans in the Middle East and symbols of the United States abroad were more convenient and accessible targets. However, with the bombing of the World Trade Center, a psychological barrier of security has been breached by the terrorists. In New Jersey and in Brooklyn, a blind shaykh raised his voice against the government of Egypt and its supporter, the United States. He condemned the "demon" called America and exhorted his followers to "destroy their edifices." That is precisely what some of Shaykh Umar Abd'Al Rahman's disciples attempted. Although the bombing of the World Trade Center was only partially successful, the "Gang That Could Not Shoot Straight" caused several hundred million dollars of damage, more than a thousand injuries, and six deaths. All this was accomplished by relatively untrained amateurs bound by an adherence to a fanatical view of Islam and a hatred for the role of the United States as the principal supporter of Israel. Foreign elements and governments are attempting to manipulate and exploit co-religionists and co-nationals in US urban environments. In the past, groups such as Hamas and the Irish Republican Army (IRA) have used the United States strictly as an arena to raise funds for their violent activities. Now, with ethnic tensions unleashed in the aftermath of the Cold War, the United States will likely become a terrorist target to the same extent that the United Kingdom is prey to the IRA, Italy to the Mafia, Egypt to the Islamic Jihad, Colombia to the drug cartels, and Turkey to Kurdish PKK.

Looking Toward the Future

Indeed, as ethnic tensions rise, terrorism will increase and adversely affect the United States and its allies. The United States is now at risk from both new and old sources of terrorism. Iran, Sudan, and other countries are encouraging the spread of terrorism from North Africa to North America. As technology proliferates and Middle Eastern nations accumulate funds, terrorism will be used as leverage against other states. There is also a new architecture of loosely directed terrorists and independent operators extending from South Asia to Europe, Central Asia, and North America.

The end of the Cold War has also accelerated unconventional warfare opportunities. Although the relationship between terrorist organizations and their former state sponsors threatened the United States during the Cold War, the political parameters within which terrorists were forced to operate tended to constrain rash and ill-considered terrorist attacks. Today's relationships are ambiguous at best, with political conflicts replaced by fervent religious, ethnic, and nationalistic struggles.

The essential question for counterterrorist experts is how the risking availability of weapons on the black market will affect future terrorism. While the question remains unanswered, we do know that weapons, some of them very sophisticated, are available on the black market. The states of the former Soviet Union need money, and they have a vested economic interest in supplying weapons throughout the world. These include not only unsophisticated weaponry like the AK-47, but also very sophisticated weaponry such as biological, chemical, and nuclear armaments. Small nations and aggressive terrorist groups are likely to be the happy recipients of such weapons.

Given the apparent instability of the post-Cold War world, it is important to determine the profiles of future terrorists. Although some members of militant extremist groups are college-trained and have advanced degrees in nuclear engineering and cybernetics, most terrorists are peasants with limited training and resources. Completing the picture even further, today's terrorism is global. Terrorist organizations, no longer receiving funds from their patrons, are turning to organized crime for revenue. Realizing the financial opportunities, some groups have abandoned their ideologies to become criminal organizations and are thereby able to afford more expensive and destructive weaponry. This growing nexus must be closely examined by intelligence and law enforcement agencies. It is also necessary for counterterrorist agencies to determine the demographic factors effecting terrorists today so we can predict what business as usual will be tomorrow. It remains unclear how and which groups are influenced by global organized crime in the aftermath of the Cold War. It is also unclear how and which terrorist groups will manipulate the information superhighway.

One trend, however, is clear – state sponsored terrorism will continue to play an active role. The danger is that state sponsors, such as Iran, can now grant terrorists access to their sophisticated technology. The Iranian Revolutionary Guard is already training the Sudanese militia according to the Iranian model and supports the training of radical Islamic activists in communities scattered throughout the world. While the techniques taught include assassinations and the use of car bombs, they may also work to devise methods that will have an even greater impact, particularly in urban Western societies. While counterterrorist technical expertise in the United States has grown, so too has the professional terrorist's ability to analyze and assess opportunities for attack. Recent urban terrorist bombings in Argentina and London are indicative of the trend.

When the dust settles, both literally and figuratively, it will become clear that the World Trade Center bombing and related events were sponsored by plausibly deniable agents of foreign governments. Iran and Iraq come to mind. Of these two, Iran is the best positioned geopolitically and logistically.

It is doubtful that "amateur terrorism" will replace state-sponsored terrorism as a tool for maintaining group visibility. Although more easily executed than state-sponsored efforts, "amateur terrorism" is much more vulnerable to intelligence and police countermeasures. Such groups will not replace sophisticated organizations. They can, however, behave as temporary irritants. Over time, amateur terrorist groups of varying sophistication will emerge. But even those most capable of garnering publicity due to their viciousness are not likely to be of great strategic consequence.

The tactics of future terrorists are as difficult to discern as the profiles of future terrorists. While I agree with Jenkins that terrorist tactics in the future will most likely be the tactics of today, I believe that we will see an acceleration of innovative changes employing more advanced technology. I suspect a number of analysts including myself, have overstated the probability of terrorists using weapons of mass destruction. What is of immediate concern, however, is that mass destruction could be caused by the use of relatively low-tech weapons against civilians and other soft targets. Had the attack on the World Trade Center been more innovative, more casualties and even greater destruction could have resulted.

The forms of terrorism we may face go beyond bombings, airplane hijacking, or hostage-taking. State-sponsored terrorists will possess far more sophisticated tools than they do presently and will be able to resolve complex logistical and communications problems. For example, multi-phase fused explosive charges are believed to have been used in the Pan Am 103 bombing. Enhanced crypto-graphy and portable satellite links will provide terrorists with secure lines of communication. There is concern that terrorist groups are using more lethal devices, but one must remember that they have used sophisticated explosives and detonating mechanisms for years. To destroy Pan Am 103, terrorists used a small amount of the plastic explosive Semtex, which is more powerful and harder to detect than traditional explosives. The provisional IRA has become expert in building bombs with long-delay timing devices that can be set to explode in weeks or months, rather than in hours. The IRA almost killed British Prime Minister Margaret Thatcher and her cabinet with such a bomb in 1985.

Over the years, analysts of terrorism have focused on the vulnerability of our infrastructure and on the possibility of terrorist groups resorting to weapons of mass destruction.

We have neglected the subtle and complex changes in international and criminal support of terrorism that will shape the coming evolution in tactics and targets. These factors are the ones which will determine how terrorists and supercriminals will make use of the information superhighway of the future, both as a tool in doing business and as a target. Indeed, the March 20, 1995 nerve gas attack in Japan's subway system highlights the fact that mass-destruction terrorism is becoming a reality. Further, the Oklahoma City bombing, ostensibly by militia members, brings terrorism right to the heartland of America.

And finally the September 11, 2001 terrorist attacks on America has totally shaken the edifice of security of American security forces forget the security of masses.

6

Anatomy of Terrorism

What is Terrorism?

The word 'terrorism was first coined during the French Revolution. In contrast to its contemporary usage, at that time terrorism had a decidedly *positive* connotation. The system or *regime de la terreur* of 1793–4 from which the English word came—was adopted as a means to establish order during the transient anarchical period of turmoil and upheaval that followed the uprisings of 1789, as it has followed in the wake of many other revolutions. Hence, unlike terrorism as it is commonly understood today, to mean a *revolutionary* or anti-government activity undertaken by no-state or subnational entities, the *regime de la terreur* was an instrument of governance wielded by the recently established revolutionary *state.* It was designed to consolidate the new government's power by intimidating counter-revolutionaries, subversives and all other dissidents whom the new regime regarded as 'enemies of the people'. The Committee of General Security and the Revolutionary Tribunal ('People's Court' in the modern vernacular were thus accorded wide powers of arrest and judgement, publicly putting to death by guillotine persons convicted of treasonous (i.e. reactionary) crimes.

Terrorism in its original context was also closely associated with the ideals of virtue and democracy. The revolutionary leader Maximilien Robespierre firmly believed that virtue was the mainspring of a popular government at peace, but that during the time of revolution must be allied with terror in order for democracy to triumph. He appealed famously to 'virtue, without which terror is evil; terror, without which virtue is helpless', and proclaimed: *'Terror is nothing but justice, prompt, severe and inflexible; it is therefore an emanation of virtue.'*

Despite this divergence from its subsequent meaning, the French Revolution's 'terrorism' still shared at least two key characteristics in common with its modern-day variant. First, the *regime de la terreur* was neither random nor indiscriminate, as terrorism is often portrayed today, but was organized, deliberate and systematic. Second, its goal and its very justification—like that of contemporary terrorism–was the creation of a 'new and better society' in place of a conventional corrupt and undemocratic political system. Indeed, Robespierre's vague and utopian exegeses of the revolution's central goals are remarkably similar in tone and content to the equally turgid, millenarian manifestos issued by many contemporary revolutionary—primarily left-wing, Marxist-oriented—terrorist organizations. For example, in 1794 Robespierre declared, in language easily presaging the communiques issued by groups such as Germany's Red Army Faction and Italy's Red Brigades nearly two centuries later:

> We want an order of things ... in which the arts are an adornment to the liberty that ennobles them, and commerce the source of *wealth for the public and not of monstrous opulence for a few families* ... In our country we desire morality instead of selfishness, honesty and not mere 'honour', principle and not mere custom, duty and not mere propriety, the sway of reason rather than the tyranny of fashion, a scorn for vice and not a contempt for the unfortunate ... (emphasis added)

Like many other revolutions, the French Revolution eventually began to consume itself. Fearing that their own names might be on that list, extremists joined forces with moderated to repudiate both Robespierre and his *regime de la terreur.* Robespierre and his closest followers themselves met the same fate that had befallen some 40,000 others: execution by guillotine. The Terror was at an end: thereafter *terrorism* became a term associated with the abuse of office and power – with overt 'criminal' implications. Within a year of Robespierre's demise, the word had been popularized in English by Edmund Burke who, in his famous polemic against the French Revolution, described the 'Thousands of those Hell hounds called Terrorists ..., let loose on the people'.

One of the French Revolution's more enduring repercussions was the impetus it gave to anti-monarchical sentiment elsewhere in Europe. Popular subservience to rulers who derived their authority from God through 'divine right of fuel', not from their subjects, was increasingly questioned by a politically awakened continent. The advent of nationalism, and with it notions of statehood and citizenship based on the common identity of a people rather than the lineage of a royal family, were resulting in the unification and creation of new nation-states such as Germany and Italy. Meanwhile, the massive socio-economic changes engendered by the industrial revolution were creating new 'universalist' ideologies (such as communism/ Marxism), born of the alienation and exploitative conditions of nineteenth-century capitalism. From this milieu a new era of terrorism emerged in which the concept had gained many of the familiar revolutionary, anti-state connotations of today. Its chief progenitor was arguably the Italian republican extremist, Carlo Pisacane, who had forsaken his birthright as duke of San Giovanni only to perish in 1857 during an ill-fated revolt against Bourbon rule. A passionate advocate of federalism and mutualism, Pisacane is remembered less on this account than for the theory of 'propaganda by deed', which he is credited with defining - an idea that has exerted a compelling influence on rebels and terrorists alike ever since. 'The propaganda of the idea is a chimera,' Pisacane wrote. 'Ideas result from deeds, not the latter from the former, and the people will not be free when they are educated, but educated when they are free.' Violence, he argued, was necessary not only to draw attention to, or generate publicity for, a cause, but to inform, educate and ultimately rally the masses behind the revolution. The didactic purpose of violence, Pisacane argued, could never be effectively replaced by pamphlets, wall posters or assemblies.

Perhaps the first organization to put into practice Pisacane's dictum was the narodnaya Volya, or People's Will (sometimes translated as People's Freedom), a small group of Russian constitutionalists that had been founded in 1878 to challenge tsarist rule. For the Narodnaya Volya, the apathy and alienation of the Russian masses afforded few alternatives to the resort to daring and dramatic acts of violence designed to attract attention to the group and its cause. However, unlike the many late twentieth-century terrorist organizations who have cited the principle of 'propaganda by deed' to justify the wanton targeting of civilians in order to assure them publicity thought the shock and horror produced by wholesale bloodshed, the Narodnaya Volya displayed an almost quixotic attitude to the violence they wrought. To them, 'propaganda by deed' meant the selective targeting of specific individuals whom the group considered the embodiment of the autocratic, oppressive state. Hence their victims–were deliberately chosen for their 'symbolic' value as the dynastic heads and subservient agents of a corrupt and tyrannical regime. An intrinsic element in the group's collective beliefs was that 'not one drop of superfluous blood' should be shed in pursuit of aims, however noble or utilitarian they might be. Even having selected their targets with great care and the utmost deliberation, group members still harboured profound regrets about taking the life of a fellow human being. Their unswerving adherence to this principle is perhaps best illustrated by the failed attempt on the life of the Grand Duke Serge Alexandrovich made by a successor organization to the Narodnaya Volya in 1905. As the royal carriage came into view, the terrorist tasked with the assassination saw that the duke was unexpectedly accompanied by his children and therefore aborted his mission rather than risk harming the intended victim's family (the duek was killed in a subsequent attack).

The Narodnaya Volya's most dramatic accomplishment also led directly to its demise. On 1 March 1881 the group assassinated Tsar Alexander II. The failure of eight previous plots had led the conspirators to take extraordinary measures to ensure the success of this attempt. Four volunteers were given four bombs each and deployed along the alternative routed followed the tsar's cortege. As two of the bomber-assassins stood in wait on the same street, the sleighs carrying the Tsar and his Cossack escort approached the first terrorist, who hurled his bomb at the passing sleigh, missing it by inches. The whole entourage came to a halt as soldiers seized the hapless culprit and the Tsar descended from his sleigh to check on a bystander wounded by the explosion. 'Thank God, I am safe,' the Tsar reportedly declared—just as the second bomber emerged from the crowd and detonated his weapon, killing both himself and his target. The full weight of the Tsarist state now fell on the heads of the Narodnaya Volya. Acting on information provided by the arrested member, the secret police swept down on the group's safe houses and hide-outs, rounding up most of the plotters, who were quickly tried, convicted and hanged. Further information from this group led to subsequent arrests, so that within a year of the assassination only one member of the original executive committee was still at large. She too was finally apprehended in 1883, at which point the first generation of Narodnaya Volya terrorists ceased to exist, although various successor organizations subsequently emerged to carry on the struggle.

At the time, the repercussions of the tsar's assassination could not have been known or appreciated by either the condemned or their comrades languishing in prison or exiled to Siberia. But in addition to the precipitating the beginning of the end of tsarist rule, the group also deeply influenced individual revolutionaries and subversive organizations elsewhere. To the nascent anarchist movement, the 'propaganda by deed' strategy championed by the Narodnaya Volya provided a model to be emulated. Within four months of the tsar's murder, a group of radicals in London convened an 'anarchist conference' which publicly applauded the assassination and extolled tyrannicide as a means to the achieve revolutionary change. In hopes of encouraging and coordinating worldwide anarchist activities, the conferees decided to establish an 'Anarchist International' (or 'Black International'). Although this idea, like most of their ambitious plans, came to nought, the publicity generated by even a putative 'Anarchist International' was sufficient to create a myth of global revolutionary pretensions and thereby stimulate fears and suspicions disproportionate to its actual impact or political achievements. Disparate and uncoordinated though the anarchists' violence was, the movement's emphasis on individual action or operations carried out by small cells of the like-minded radicals made detection and prevention by the police particularly difficult, thus further heightening public fears. For example, following the assassination of US President William McKinley in 1901 (by a young Hungarian refugee, Leon Czolgocz, who, while not a regular member of any anarchist organization, was nonetheless influenced by the philosophy), Congress swiftly enacted legislation barring known anarchists or anyone 'who disbelieves in or is opposed to all organized government' from entering the United Sates. However, while anarchists were responsible for an impressive string of assassinations of heads of state and a number of particularly notorious bombings from about 1878 until the second decade of the twentieth century, in the final analysis, other than stimulating often exaggerated fears, anarchism made little tangible impact on either the domestic or the international politics of the countries affected. It does, however, offer an interesting historical footnote: much as the 'information revolution' of the late twentieth century is alleged to have made the means and methods of bomb-making and other types of terrorist activity more readily available via the Internet, on CD-ROM, and through ordinary libraries and bookstores, one of anarchism's flourishing 'cottage industries' more than a century earlier was the widespread distribution of similar 'how-to' manuals and publications of violence and mayhem.

On the eve of the World War I, terrorism still retained its revolutionary connotations. By this time, growing unrest and irredentist ferment had already welled up within the decaying Ottoman and Habsburg Empires. In the 1880s and 1890s, for example, militant Armenian nationalist movements in eastern Turkey pursued a terrorist strategy against continued Ottoman rule of a kind that would later be adopted by most of the post-World War II ethnonationalist/separatist movements. The Armenians' objective was simultaneously to strike a blow against the despotic 'alien' regime through repeated attacks on its colonial administration and security forces, in order to rally indigenous support, as well as to attract international attention, sympathy and support. Around the same time, the Inner Macedonian Revolutionary Organization (IMRO) was active in the region overlapping present-day Greece, Bulgaria and Serbia. Although the Macedonians did not go on to suffer the catastrophic fate that befell the Armenians during the World War II (when an estimated one million persons died in what is considered to be the first officially implemented genocide of the twentieth century), IMRO never came close to achieving its aim of an independent Macedonia and thereafter degenerated into a mostly criminal organization of hired thugs and political assassins.

The events immediately preceding the World War I in Bosnia are of course more familiar because of their subsequent cataclysmic impact on world affairs. There, similar groups of disaffected nationalists—Bosnaian Serb intellectuals, university students and even schoolchildren, collectively known as Mlada Bosnia, or Young Bosnians - arose against continued Habsburg suzerainty. While it is perhaps easy to dismiss the movement, as some historians have as comprised of 'frustrated, poor, dreary and maladjusted' adolescents-much as many contemporary observers similarly denigrate modern-day terrorists as mindless, obsessive and maladjusted—it was a member of Young Bosnia, Gavrilo Princip, who is widely credited with having set in motion the chain of events that began on 28 June 1914, when he assassinated the Habsburg Archduke Franz Ferdinand in Sarajevo, and culminated in the First World War. Whatever its superficially juvenile characteristics, the group was nonetheless passionately dedicated to the attainment of a federal South Slav political entity—uniting Solvenes, Croats and Serbs—and resolutely committed to assassination as the vehicle with which to achieve that aim. In this respect, the Young Bosnians perhaps had more in common with the radical republicanism of Giuseppe Mazzini, one of the most ardent exponents of Italian unification in the nineteenth century, than with groups such as the Narodnaya Volya—despite a shared conviction in the efficacy of tyrannicide. An even more significant difference, however, was the degree of involvement in, and external support provided to, Young Bosnian activities by various shadowy Serbian nationalist groups. Principal among these was the pan-Serb secret society, the Narodna Obrana ('The People's Defence' or 'National Defence').

The Narodna Obrana had been established in 1908 originally to promote Serb cultural and national activities. It subsequently assumed a more subversive orientation as the movement became increasingly involved with anti-Austrian activities – including terrorism – mostly in neighbouring Bosnia and Hercegovina. Although the Narodna Obrana's exclusionist pan-Serbian aims clashed with the Young Bosnian's less parochial South Slav ideals, its leadership was quite happy to manipulate and exploit the Bosnians' emotive nationalism and youthful zeal for their own purposes. To this end, the Narodna Obrana actively recruited, trained and armed young Bosnians and Hercegovinians from movements such as the Young Bosnians who were then deployed in various seditious activities against the Habsburgs. As early as four years before the Archduke's assassination, a Hercegovinian Youth, trained by a Serb army officer with close ties to the Narodna Obrana, had attempted to kill the governor of Bosnia. But, while the Narodna Obrana included among its members senior Serbian government officials, it was not an explicitly government-controlled or directly state-supported activity. Whatever hazy government links it maintained were further and deliberately obscured when a radical faction left the Narodna Obrana in 1911 and established the Ujedinjenje ili Smrt, 'The Union of Death' or 'Death or Unification' - ore popularly known as the Crna Ruka, or the 'Black Hand'.

This group, which continued to maintain close links with its parent body, was largely composed of serving Serbian military officers. It was led by Lieutenant-Colonel Dragutin Dmitrievich (known by his pseudonym, Apis) himself the chief of the Intelligence Department of the Serbian general staff. With this key additional advantage of direct access to military armaments, intelligence and training facilities, the Black Hand effectively took charge of all Serb-backed clandestine operations in Bosnia.

Although, there were obviously close links between the Serbian military, the Black Hand and the Young Bosnians, it would be a mistake to regard the relationship as one of direct control, much less outright manipulation. Clearly, the Serbian government was well aware of the Black Hand's objectives and the violent means the group employed in pursuit of them; indeed, the Serbian Crown Prince Alexander was one of the group's benefactors. But this does not mean that the Serbian government was necessarily as committed to war with Austria as the Black Hand's leaders were, or that it was prepared to countenance the group's more extreme plans for fomenting cross-border, anti-Habsburg terrorism. There is some evidence to suggest that the Black Hand may have been trying to force Austria's hand against Serbia and thereby plunge both countries into war by actively abetting the Young Bosnians' plot to assassinate the archduke. Indeed, according toone revisionist account of the events leading up to the murder, even though the pistol used by Princip had been supplied by the Black Hand from a Serb military armoury in Kragujevac, and even though Princip had been trained by the Black Hand in Serbia before being smuggled back across the border for the assassination, at the eleventh hour Dmitrievich had apparently bowed to intense government pressure and tried to stop the assassination. According to this version, Princip and his fellow conspirators would hear nothing of it and stubbornly went ahead with their plans. contrary to popular assumption, therefore, the archduke's assassination may not have been specifically ordered or even directly sanctioned by the Serbian government. However, the obscure links between high government officials and their senior military commanders and ostensibly independent, transnational terrorist movements, and the tangled web of intrigue, plots, clandestine arms provision and training, intelligence agents and cross-border sanctuary these relationships inevitably involved, provide a pertinent historical parallel to the contemporary phenomenon known as 'state-sponsored' terrorism (that is, the active and often clandestine support, encouragement and assistance provided by a foreign government to a terrorist group), which is discussed below.

By the 1930s, the meaning of 'terrorism' has changed again. It was now used less to refer to revolutionary movements and violence directed against governments and their leaders, and mode to describe the practices of mass repression employed by totalitarian states and their dictatorial leaders against their own citizens. Thus, the term regained its former connotations of *abuse of power by governments,* and was applied specifically to the *authoritarian regimes* that had come to power in Fascist Italy, Nazi Germany and Stalinist Russia. In Germany and Italy respectively, the accession to office of Hitler and Mussolini had depended in large measure on the 'street'–the mobilization and deployment of gangs of brown-or black-shirted thugs to harass and intimidate political opponents and root out other scapegoats for public vilification and further victimization. 'Terror? Never,' Mussolini insisted, demurely dismissing such intimidation as 'simply . . . social hygiene, taking those individuals out of circulation like a doctor would take out a bacilus'. The most sinister dimension of this form of 'terror' was that it became an intrinsic component of Fascist and Nazi governance, executed at the behest of and in complete subservience to, the ruling political party of the land–which had arrogated to itself complete, total control of the country and its people. A system of government-sanctioned fear and coercion was thus created whereby political brawls, street fights and widespread persecution of Jews, communists and other declared 'enemies of the state' became the means through which complete and submissive compliance was ensured.

The 'Great Terror' that Stalin was shortly to unleash in Russia both resembled and differed from that of the Nazis. On the one hand, drawing inspiration from Hitler's ruthless elimination of his own political opponents, the Russian dictator similarly transformed the political party he led into a servile instrument responsive directly to his personal will, and the state's police and security apparatus into slavish organs of coercion, enforcement and repression. But conditions in the Soviet Union of the 1930s bore little resemblance to the turbulent political, social and economic upheaval afflicting Germany and Italy during that decade and the previous one. On the other hand, therefore, unlike either the Nazis or the Fascist, who had emerged from the political free-for-alls in their own countries to seize power and then had to struggle to consolidate their rule and retain their unchallenged authority, the Russian Communist Party had by the mid-1930s been firmly entrenched in power for more than a decade. Thus the political purges ordered by Stalin became, in the words, of one of his biographers, a 'conspiracy to seize total power by terrorist action', resulting in the death, exile, imprisonment of millions.

Certainly, similar forms of state-imposed or state-directed violence and terror against a government's own citizens continue today. The use of so-called 'death squads' (often off-duty or plain-clothes security or police officers) in conjunction with blatant intimidation of political opponents, human rights and aid workers, student groups, labour organizers, journalists and others has been a prominent feature of the right-wing military dictatorships that took power in Argentina, Chile and Greece during the 1970s and even of elected governments in el Salvador, Guatemala, Colombia and Peru since the mid-1980s. But these state-sanctioned or explicitly ordered acts of *internal* political violence directed mostly against domestic populations – that is, rule by violence and intimidation by those *already* in power against their own citizenry–are generally termed 'terror' in order to distinguish that phenomenon from 'terrorism', which is understood to be violence committed by non-state entities.

Following the World War II in another swing of the pendulum of meaning, 'terrorism' regained the revolutionary connotations with which is it most commonly associated today. At that time, the term was used primarily in reference to the violent revolts then being prosecuted by the various indigenous nationalist/anti-conoialist groups that emerged in Asia, Africa and the Middle East during the late 1940s ad 1950s to oppose continued European rule. Countries as diverse as Isreael, Kenya, Cyprus and Algeria, for example, owe their independence at least in part to nationalist political movements that employed terrorism against colonial powers. It was also during this period that the 'politically correct' appellation of 'freedom fighters' came into fashion as a result of the political legitimacy that the international community (whose sympathy and support was actively courted by many of these movements) accorded to struggles for national liberation and self-determination. Many newly independent Third World countries and communist bloc states in particular adopted this vernacular, arguing that anyone or any movement that fought against 'colonial' oppression and/or Western domination should not be described as 'terrorists', but were properly deemed to be 'freedom fighters'. This position was perhaps most famously explained by the Palestine Liberation Organization (PLO) chairman Yassir Arafat, when he addressed the United Nations General Assembly in November 1974. 'The difference between the revolutionary and the terrorist,' Arafat stated, 'lies in the reason for which each fights. For whoever stands by a just cause and fights for the freedom and liberation of his land from the invaders, the settlers and the colonialists, cannot possibly be called terrorist ...' during the late 1960s and 1970s, terrorism continued to be viewed within a revolutionary context. However, this usage was expanded to include nationalist and ethnic separatist groups outside a colonial or neo-colonial framework as well as radical, entirely ideologically motivated organizations. Disenfranchised or exiled nationalist minorities–such as the PLO, the Quebecois separatist group FLQ (Front de Liberation du Quebec), the Baseue ETA (Euskadi ta Askatasuna, or Freedom for the Basque Homeland) and even a hitherto unknown South Moluccan irredentist group seeking independence from Indonesia-adopted terrorism as a means to draw attention to themselves and their respective causes, in many instances with the specific aim, like their anti-colonial predecessors, of attracting international sympathy and support. Around the same time, various left-wing political extremists – drawn mostly from the radical student organizations and Marxist/Leninist/Maoist movements in Western Europe, Latin America and the United States – began to form terrorist groups opposing American intervention in Vietnam and what they claimed were the irredeemable social and economic inequities of the modern capitalist liberal-democratic state. Although the revolutionary cum ethno-nationalist/separatist and ideological exemplars continue to shape our most basic understanding of the term, in recent years 'terrorist' has been used to denote broader, less distinct phenomena. In the early 1980s, for example, terrorism came to be regarded as a calculated means to destabilize the West as part of a vast global conspiracy. By the middle of the decade, however, a series of suicide bombings directed mostly against American diplomatic and military targets in the Middle East was focusing attention on the rising threat of state-sponsored terrorism. Consequently, this phenomenon – whereby various renegade foreign governments such as the regimes in Iran, Iraq, Libya and Syria became actively involved in sponsoring or commissioning terrorist acts – replaced communist conspiracy theories as the main context within which terrorism was viewed. Terrorism thus became associated with a type of covert or surrogate warfare whereby weaker states could confront larger, more powerful rivals without the risk of retribution.

In the early 1990s the meaning and usage of term 'terrorism' were further blurred by the emergence of two new buzzwords: 'narco-terrorism' and the so-called 'gray area phenomenon'. The former term revived the Moscoworchestrated terrorism conspiracy theories of previous years while introducing the critical new dimension of narcotics trafficking. Thus 'narco-terrorism' was defined by one of the concept's foremost propagators as the 'use or drug trafficking to advance the objectives of certain governments and terrorist organizations' – identified as the 'Marxist-Leninist regimes' of the soviet Union, Cuba, Bulgaria and Nicaragua, among others. The emphasis on 'narco-terrorism' as the latest manifestation of the communist plot to undermine Western society, however, had the unfortunate effect of diverting official attention away from a bona fide emerging trend. To a greater extent than ever in the past, entirely criminal (that is, violent, *economically* motivated) organizations were now forging strategic alliances with terrorist and guerrilla organizations or themselves employing violence for specifically political ends. The growing power of the Colombian cocaine cartels, their close ties with left-wing terrorist groups in Colombia and Peru, and their repeated attempts to subvert Colombia's electoral process and undermine successive governments constitute perhaps the best-known example of this continuing trend.

Those who drew attention to this 'gray area phenomenon' were concerned less with grand conspiracies than with highlighting the increasingly fluid and variable nature of subnational conflict in the post-Cold War era. Accordingly, i the 1990s terrorism began to be subsumed by some analysts within the gray area phenomenon'. Thus the latter term came to be used to denote 'threats to the stability of nation states by non-state actors and non-governmental processes and organizations'; to describe violence affecting 'immense regions or urban areas where control has shifted from legitimate governments to new half-political, half-criminal powers'; or simply to group together in one category the range of conflicts across the world that no longer conformed to traditionally accepted notions of war as fighting between the armed forces of two or more established states, but instead involved irregular forces as one or more of the combatants.

Dilemmas in Terrorism

Not surprisingly, as the meaning and usage of the world have changed over time to accommodate the political vernacular and discourse of each successive era, terrorism has proved increasingly elusive in the face of attempts to construct one consistent definition. At one time, the terrorists themselves were far more cooperative in this endeavour than they are today. The early practitioners didn't mince their words or hide behind the semantic camouflage of more anodyne labels such as 'freedom fighter' or 'urban guerrilla'. The nineteenth-century anarchists, for example, unabashedly proclaimed themselves to be terrorists and frankly proclaimed their tactics to be terrorism. The members of narodnaya Volya similarly displayed no qualms in using these same words to describe themselves and their deeds. However, such frankness did not last. The Jewish terrorist group of the 1940s known as Lehi (the Hebrew acronym for Lohamei Herut Yisrael, the Freedom Fighters for Israel, more popularly known simply as the Stern Gang after their founder and first leader, Abraham Stern) is thought to be one of the last terrorist groups actually to describe itself publicly as such. It is significant, however, that even Lehi, while it may have been far more candid than its latter-day counterparts, chose as the name of the organization not 'Terrorist Fighters for Israel', but the far less pejorative 'Freedom Fighters for Israel'. Similarly, although more than twenty years later the Brazilian revolutionary Carlos Marighela displayed few compunctions about openly advocating the use of 'terrorist' tactics, he still insisted on depicting himself and his disciples as 'urban guerrillas' rather than 'urban terrorists'. Indeed, it is clear from Marighela's writings that he was well aware of the word's undesirable connotations, and strove to displace them with positive resonances. To be called an aggressor or a terrorist in Brazil is now an honour to any citizen, for it means that he is fighting, with a gun in his hand, against the monstrosity of the present dictatorship and the suffering it causes.

This trend towards ever more convoluted semantic obfuscations to side-step terrorism's pejorative overtones has, if anything, become more entrenched in recent decades. Terrorist organizations almost without exception now regularly select names for themselves that consciously eschew the word 'terrorism' in any of its forms. Instead these groups actively seek to evoke images of:

(a) freedom and liberation (e.g. the National Liberation Front, the Popular Front for the Liberation of Palestine, Freedom for the Baseue Homeland, etc.);

(b) armies or other military organizational structures (e.g. the National Military Organization, the Popular Liberation Army, The Fifth Battalion of the Liberation Army, etc.);

(c) actual self-defence movements (e.g. the Afrikaner Resistance Movement, the Shankhill Defence Association, The Organization for the Defence of the Free People, the Jewish Defense Organization, etc.);

(d) righteous vengeance (the Organization for the Oppressed on Earth, the Justice Commandos of the Armenian Genocide, the Palestinian Revenge Organization, etc.).

- or else deliberately choose names that are decidedly neutral and therefore bereft of all but the most innocuous suggestions or associations (e.g. the Shining Path, Front Line, al-Dawa ('The Call'), Alfaro Live – Damn it!, Kach ('Thus'), al-Gamat al-Islamiya ('The Islamic Organization'), the Lantero Youth Movement, etc.)

What all these examples suggest is that terrorists clearly do not see or regard themselves as others do. 'Above all I am a family man,' the arch-terrorist Carlos, 'The Jackal', described himself to a French newspaper following his capture in 1994. Cast perpetually on the defensive and forced to take up arms to protect themselves and their real or imagined constituents only, terrorists perceive themselves as reluctant warriors, driven by desperation - and lacking any viable alternative - to violence against a repressive state, a predatory rival ethnic or nationalist group, or an unresponsive international order. This perceived characteristic of self-denial also distinguishes the terrorist from other types of political extremists as well as from persons similarly involved in illegal, violent avocations. A communist or a revolutionary, for example, would likely readily accept and admit that he is in fact a communist or a revolutionary. Indeed, many would doubtless take particular pride in claiming either of those appellations for themselves. Similarly, even a person engaged in illegal, wholly disreputable or entirely selfish violent activities, such as robbing banks or carrying out contract killings, would probably admit to being a bank robber or a murderer for hire. The terrorist, by contrast, will never acknowledge that he is a terrorist and moreover will go to great lengths to evade and obscure any such inference or connection. Terry Anderson, the American journalist who was held hostage for almost sever years by the Lebanese terrorist organization Hezbollah, relays a telling conversation he had with one of his guards. The guard had objected to a newspaper article that referred to Hezbollah as terrorists. 'We are not terrorists,' he indignantly stated, 'we are fighters.' Anderson replied, 'Hajj, you are a terrorist, look it up in the dictionary. You are a terrorist, you may not like the word and if you do not like the word, do not do it. The terrorist will always argue that its is society or government or the socio-economic 'system' and its laws that are the *real* 'terrorists', and moreover that if it were not for this oppression, he would not have felt the need to defend either himself or the population he claims to represent. Another revealing example of this process of obfuscation-projection may be found in the book *Invisible Armies,* written by Sheikh Muhammad Hussein Fadlallah, the spiritual leader of the Lebanese terrorist group responsible for Anderson's kidnapping. 'We don't see ourselves as terrorists,' Fadlallah explains, 'because we don't believe in terrorism. We don't see resisting the occupier as a terrorist action. We see ourselves as *mujihadeen* [holy warriors] who fight a Holy War for the people.

On one point, at least, everyone agrees: terrorism is a pejorative term. It is a word with intrinsically negative connotations that is generally applied to one's enemies and opponents, or to those with whom one disagrees and would otherwise prefer to ignore. 'What is called terrorism', Brian jenkins has written, 'thus seems to depend on one's point of view. Use of the term implies a moral judgement; and if one party can successfully attach the label *terrorist* to its opponent, then it has indirectly persuaded others to adopt its moral viewpoint.' Hence the decision to call someone or bale some organization 'terrorist' becomes almost unavoidably subjective depending largely on whether one sympathizes with or opposes the person/group/cause concerned. If one identifies with the victim of the violence, for example, then the act its terrorism. If, however, one identifies with the perpetrator, the violent act is regarded in a more sympathetic, if not positive (or, at the worst, an ambivalent light; and it is not terrorism.

The implications of this associational logic were perhaps most clearly demonstrated in the exchanges between Eastern and no-Western member states of the United Nations following the 1972 Munich Olympics massacre, in which eleven Israeli athletes were killed. The debate began with the proposal by the then UN Secretary-General, Kurt Waldheim, that the UN should not remain a 'mute spectator' to the acts of terrorist violence then occurring throughout the world but should take practical steps that might prevent further bloodshed. While a majority of the UN member states supported the Secretary-General, a disputatious minority - including many Arab states and various African and Asian countries - derailed the discussion, arguing (much as Arafat would do two years later in his own address to the General Assembly) that 'people who struggle to liberate themselves from foreign oppression and exploitation have the right to use all methods at their disposal, including force.'

The Third World War delegates justified their position with two arguments. First, they claimed that all bona fide liberation movements are invariably decried as 'terrorists' by the regimes against which their struggles for freedom are directed. The Nazis, for example, labelled as terrorists the resistance groups opposing Germany's occupation of their lands, Moulaye el-Hassen, the Mauritanian ambassador, pointed out, just as 'all liberation movements are described as terrorists by those who have deduced them to slavery'. Therefore, by condemning 'terrorism' the UN was endorsing the power of the strong over the weak and of the established entity over its no-established challenger - in effect, acting as the defender of the status quo. According to Chen Chu, the deputy representative of the People's Republic of China, the UN thus was proposing to deprive 'oppressed nationals and people's of the only effective weapon they had with which to oppose 'imperialism, colonialism, neo-cononialism, racism and Israeli Zionism'. Second the Third World delegates argues forcefully that it is not the violence itself that is germane, but its 'underlying causes': that is, the 'misery, frustration, grievance and despair' that produce the violent acts. As the Mauritanian representative again explained, the term 'terrorist' could 'hardly be held to apply to persons who were denied the most elementary human rights, dignity, freedom and independence, and whose countries objected to foreign occupation'. When the issue was again raised the following year, Syria objected on the grounds that 'the international community is under legal and moral obligation to promote the struggle for liberation and to resist any attempt to depict this struggle as synonymous with terrorism and illegitimate violence'. The resultant definitional paralysis subsequently throttled UN efforts to make any substantive progress on international cooperation against terrorism beyond very specific agreements on individual aspects of the problem (concerning, for example, diplomats and civil aviation).

The appositive approach, where identification with the victim determines the classification of a violent act as terrorism, is evident in the conclusions of a parliamentary working group NATO (an organization comprised of long-established, status quo Western states). The final report of the 1989 North Atlantic Assembly's Subcommittee on Terrorism states: 'Murder, kidnapping, arson and other felonious acts constitute criminal behavior, but many non-Western nationals have proved reluctant to condemn as terrorist acts what they consider to be struggles of national liberation.' In this reasoning the defining characteristic of terrorism is the act of violence itself, not the motivations or justification for or reasons behind it. This approach has long been espoused by analysts such as Jenkins who argue that terrorism should be defined 'by the nature of the act, not by the identity of the perpetrators or the nature of their cause'. But this is not an entirely satisfactory solution either, since it fails to differentiate clearly between violence perpetrated by states and by no-state entities, such as terrorists. Accordingly, it plays into the hands of terrorists and their apologists who would argue that there is no difference between the 'low-tech' terrorist pipe-bomb placed in the rubbish bin at a crowded market that wantonly and indiscriminately kills or maims everyone within a radius measured in tens of feet and the 'high-tech' precision-guided ordnance dropped by air force fighter-bombers from a height of 20,000 feet or more that achieves the same wanton and indiscriminate effects on the crowded marketplace far below. The rationale thus equates the random violence inflicted on enemy population centres by military forces – such as the Luftwaffe's raids on Warswaw and Coventry, the Allied fire-bombings of Dresden and Tokyo, and the atomic bombs dropped by the United States on Hiroshima and Nagasaki during the World war II, and indeed the countervalue strategy of the post-war superpowers' strategic nuclear policy, which deliberately targeted the enemy's civilian population – with the violence committed by substate entities labelled 'terrorists', since both involve the infliction of death and injury on non-combatants. Indeed, this was precisely the point made during the above-mentioned UN debates by the Cuban representative, who argued that 'the methods of combat used by national liberation movements could not be declared illegal while the policy of terrorism unleashed against certain peoples [by the armed forces established states] was declared legitimate'.

It is familiar argument. Terrorists, as we have seen, deliberately cloak themselves in the terminology of military jargon. They consciously portray themselves as bona fide (freedom) fighters, if not soldiers, who – though they wear no identifying uniform or insignia – are entitled to treatment as prisoners of war (POWs) if captured and therefore should not be prosecuted as common criminals in ordinary courts of law. Terrorists further argue that, because of their numerical inferiority, far more limited firepower and paucity of resources compared with an established nation-state's massive defence and national security apparatus, they have no choice but to operate clandestinely, emerging from the shadows to carry out dramatic (in other words, bloody and destructive) acts of hit-and-run violence in order to attract attention to, and ensure publicity for, themselves and their cause. The bomb-in-the-rubbish-bin, in their view, is merely a circumstantially imposed 'poor man's air force': the only means with which the terrorist can challenge – and get the attention of – the more powerful state. 'How else can we bring pressure to bear on the world?' One of Arafat's political aides once enquired. 'The deaths are regrettable, they are no more innocent than the Palestinian women and children killed by the Israelis and we are ready to carry the war all over the world.'

But rationalizations such as these ignore the fact that, even while national armed forces have been responsible for far more death and destruction than terrorists might ever aspire to bring about, there nonetheless is a fundamental qualitative difference between the two types of violence. Even in war there are rules and accepted norms of behaviour that prohibit the use of certain types of weapons (for example, hollow-point or 'dum-dum' bullets, CS 'tear' gas, chemical and biological warfare agents), proscribe various tactics and outlaw attacks on specific categories of targets. Accordingly, in theory, if not always in practice, the rules of war – as observed from the early seventeenth century when they were first proposed by the Dutch jurist Hugo Grotius and subsequently codified in the famous Geneva and Hague Conventions on Warfare of the 1860s, 1899, 1907 and 1949 – not only grant civilian non-combatants immunity from attack, but also

- prohibit taking civilians as hostages;
- impose regulations governing the treatment of captured or surrendered soldiers (POWs);
- outlaw reprisals against either civilians or POWs;
- recognize neutral territory and the rights of citizens of neutral states; and
- uphold the inviolability of diplomats and other accredited representatives.

Even the most cursory review of terrorist tactics and targets over the past quarter-century reveals that terrorists have violated all these rules. They not infrequently have

- taken hostage civilians, whom in some instances they have then brutally executed (e.g. the former Italian prime minister Aldo Moro and the German industrialist Hans martin Schleyer, who were respectively taken captive and later murdered by the Red Brigades and the Red Army Faction);
- similarly abused and murdered kidnapped military officers – even when they were serving on UN-sponsored peacekeeping or truce supervisory missions (e.g. the American Marine Lieutenant-Colonel William Higgins, the commander of a UN truce monitoring detachment, who was abducted by Lebanese Shi'a terrorists in 1989 and subsequently hanged);
- undertaken reprisals against wholly innocent civilians, often in countries far removed from the terrorist's ostensible 'theatre of operation', thus disdaining any concept of neutral states or the rights of citizens of neutral countries (e.g. the brutal 1986 machine-gun and hand-grenade attack on Turkish Jewish worshippers at an Istanbul synagogue carried out by the Palestinian Abu Nidal Organization in retaliation for a recent Israeli raid on a guerrilla base in southern Lebanon); and
- repeatedly attacked embassies and other diplomatic installations (e.g. the bombings of the US embassies in Beirut and Kuwait City in 1983 and 1984, and the mass hostage-taking at the Japanese ambassador's residence in Lima, Peru, in 1996-7), as well as deliberately targeting diplomats and other accredited representatives (e.g. the British ambassador to Uruguary, Sir Geoffrey Jackson, who was kidnapped by leftist terrorists in that country in 1971, and the fifty-two American diplomats taken hostage at the Tehran legation in 1979).

Admittedly, the armed forces of established states have also been guilty of violating some of the same rules of war. However, when these transgressions do occur – when civilians are deliberately and wantonly attacked in war or taken hostage and killed by military forces – the term 'war crime' is used to describe such acts and, imperfect and flawed as both international and national judician remedies may be, steps nonetheless are often taken to hold the perpetrates accountable for these crimes. By comparison, one of the fundamental *raisons d'etre of* international terrorism is a refusal to be bound by such rules of warfare and codes of conduct. International terrorism disdains any concept of delimited areas of combat or demarcated battlefields, much less respect of neutral territory. Accordingly, terrorists have repeatedly taken their often parochial struggles to other, sometimes geographically distant, third party countries and there deliberately enmeshed persons completely unconnected with the terrorists' cause or grievances in violent incidents designed to generate attention and publicity.

The reporting of terrorism by the news media, which have been drawn into the semantic debates that divided the UN in the 1970s and continue to influence all discourse on terrorism, has further contributed to the obfuscation of the terrorist/'freedom fighter' debate, enshrining imprecision and implication as the ligua franca of political violence in the name of objectivity and neutrality. In striving to avoid appearing either partisan or judgemental, the American media, for example, resorted to describing rettorists – often in the same report – as variously guerrillas, gunmen, raiders, commandos and even soldiers. A random sample of American newspaper reports of Palestinian terrorist activities between June and December 1973, found in the terrorism archives and database maintained at the University of St Andrews in Scotland, provided striking illustrations of this practice. Out of eight headlines of articles describing the same incident, six used the word 'guerrillas' and only two 'terrorists' to describe the perpetrators. An interesting pattern was also observed whereby those accounts that immediately followed a particularly horrific or tragic incident – that is, involving the death and injury of innocent persons (in this instance, the attack on a Pan Am airliner at Rome airport, in which thirty-two passengers were killed) – tended to describe the perpetrates as 'terrorists' and their act as 'terrorism' (albeit in one case only in the headline, before reverting to the more neutral terminology of 'commando', 'militants', and 'guerrilla attack' in the text) more frequently than did reports of less serious or non-lethal incidents. The *Christian Science Monitor's* reports of the Rime Pan Am attack similarly avoided 'terrorist' and 'terrorism' in favour of 'guerrillas' and 'extremists'; an Associated Press story in the next day's *Los Angeles Times* also struck with 'guerrillas', while the two *Washington Post* articles on the same incident opted for the terms 'commandos' and 'guerrillas'.

This slavish devotion to terminological neutrality, which David Rapoport first observed over twenty years ago, is still in evidence today. A recent article appearing in the *International Herald Tribune* (a [aros-based newspaper published in conjunction with the *New York Times* and *Washington Post)* reported an incident in Algeria where thirty persons had been killed by perpetrater who were variously described as 'terrorists' in the article's headline, less judgementally as 'extremists' in the lead paragraph and as the still more ambiguous 'Islamic fundamentalists' in the article's third paragraph. In a country that since 1992 has been afflicted with an unrelenting wave of terrorist violence and bloodshed that has claimed the lives of an estimated 75,000 persons, one might think that the distinctions between 'terrorists', mere 'extremists' and ordinary 'fundamentalist' would be clearer. Equally interesting was the article that appeared on the opposite side of the same page of the newspaper that described the 'decades of sporadi *guerrilla* warfare by the IRA' in Northern Ireland. Yet fifty years ago the same newspaper apparently had fewer qualms about using the word 'terrorists' to describe the two young Jewish men in pre-independence Israel who, while awaiting execution after having been convicted of attacking British military targets, committed suicide. Other press accounts of the same period in *The Times* of London and the *Palestine Post* similarly had no difficulties, for example, in describing the 1946 bombing by Jewish terrorists of the British military headquarters and government secretariat located in the Jerusalem's King David Hotel as a 'terrorist' act perpetrated by 'terrorists'. Similarly, in perhaps the most specific application of the term, the communist terrorists against whom the British fought in Malaya throughout the late 1940s and 1950s were routinely referred to as 'CTs' – for 'Communist terrorists'. As Rapoport warned in the 1970s, 'In attempting to correct the abuse of language for political purposes, our journalists may succeed in making language altogether worthless.

The cumulative effect of this proclivity towards equivocation is that today there is not one widely accepted or agreed definition for terrorism. Different departments or agencies of even the same government will themselves often have very different definitions for terrorism. The US State Department, for example, uses the definition of terrorism contained in Title 22 of the United Sates Code, Section 2656f(d):

> premeditated, politically motivated violence perpetrated against noncombatant targets by subnational groups or clandestine agents, usually intended to influence an audience,

while the US Federal Bureau of Investigation (FBI) defines terrorism as

> the unlawful use of the force of violence against persons or property to intimidate or coerce a Government, the civilian population, or any segment thereof, in furtherance of political or social objectives,

and the US Department of Defense defines it as

> the unlawful use of – or threatened use of – force or violence against individuals or property to coerce or intimidate governments or societies, often to achieve political, religious, or ideological objectives.

Not surprisingly, each of the above definitions reflects the priorities and particular interests of the specific agency involved. The State Department's emphasis is on the premeditated and planned or calculated nature of terrorism in contrast to more spontaneous acts of political violence. Its definition is also the only one of the three to emphasize both the ineluctably political nature of terrorism and the perpetrators. fundamental 'subnational' characteristic. The State Department definition, however, is conspicuously deficient in failing to consider the psychological dimension of terrorism. Terrorism is as much about the threat of violence as the violent act itself and, accordingly, is deliberately conceived to have far-reaching psychological repercussions beyond the actual target of the act among a wider, watching, 'target' audience. As Jenkins succinctly observed two decades ago, 'Terrorism is theatre.'

Given the FBI's mission of investigating and solving crimes – both political (e.g. terrorism) and other – it is not surprising that its definition focuses on different elements. Unlike the State Department, this definition does address the psychological dimensions of the terrorist act described above, laying stress on terrorism's intimidatory and coercive aspects. The FBI definition also identified a much morader category of terrorist targets than only 'noncombatants', specifying not only governments and their citizens but also inanimate objects, such as private and public property. The FBI definition further recognizes social alongside political objectives as fundamental terrorist aims – though it offers no clearer elucidation of either.

It is not only individual agencies within the same governmental apparatus that cannot agree on a single definition of terrorism. [Experts and other long-established scholars in the field are equally incapable of reaching a consensus. In the first edition of his magisterial survey, *Political Terrorism: A Research Guide,* Alex Schmid devoted more than a hundred pages to examining more than a hundred different definitions of terrorism in an effort to discover a broadly acceptable, reasonably comprehensive explication of the word. Four years and a second edition later, Schmid was no closer to the goal of his quest, conceding in the first sentence of the revised volume that the 'search for an adequate definition is still on'. Walter Laqeur despaired of defining terrorism in both editions of his monumental work on the subject, maintaining that it is neither possible to do so not worthwhile to make the attempt. 'Ten years of debates on typologies and definitions', he responded to a survey on definitions conducted by Schmid, 'have not enhanced our knowledge of the subject to a significant degree.' Laqueur's contention is supported by the twenty-two different word categories occurring in the 109 different definitions that Schmid identified in his survey] (see Table 1 overleaf)

At the end of this exhaustive exercise, Schmid asks 'whether the above list contains all the elements necessary for a good definition. The answer', he suggests, 'is probably "no".' If it is impossible to define terrorism, as Laqueur argues, and fruitless to attempt to cobble together a truly comprehensive definition, as Schmid admits, are we to conclude that terrorism is pmpervious to precise, much less accurate definition? Not entirely. If we cannot define terrorism, then we can at least usefully distinguish it from other types of violence and identify the characteristics that make terrorism the distinct phenomenon of political violence that it is.

Types of Terrorism

Guerilla warfare is a good place to start. Terrorism is often confused or equated with, or treated as synonymous with, guerrilla warfare. This is not entirely surprising, since guerrillas often employ the same tactics (assassination, kidnapping, bombing of public gathering-places, hostage-taking, etc.) for the same purposes (to intimidate or coerce, thereby affecting behaviour through the arousal of fear) as terrorists. In addition, both terrorists and guerrillas wear neither uniform not identifying insignia and thus are often indistinguishable from non-combatants. 'Guerrilla', for example, in its most widely accepted usage, is taken to refer to a numerically larger group of armed individuals, who operate as a military unit, attack enemy military forces, and seize and hold territory while also exercising some form of sovereignty or control over a defined geographical area and its population. Terrorists, however, do not function in the open as armed units, generally do not attempt to seize or hold territory, deliberately avoid engaging enemy military forces in combat and rarely exercise any direct control or sovereignty either over territory or population.

Terrorists and Criminals

Like terrorists, criminals use violence as a means to attaining a specific end. However, while the violent act itself may be similar - kidnapping, shooting, arson, for example - the purpose or motivation clearly is not. Whether the criminal employs violence as a means to obtain money, to acquire material goods, or to kill or injure a specific victim for pay, he is acting primarily for selfish, personal motivations (usually material gain). Moreover, unlike terrorism, the ordinary criminal's violent act is not designed or intended to have consequences or create psychological repercussions beyond the act itself. The criminal may of course use some short-term act of violence to 'terrorize' his victim, such as waving a gun in the face of a bank clerk during a robbery in order to ensure the clerk's expeditious compliance. In these instances, however, the bank robber is conveying no

Frequencies of Definitional Elements in 109 Definitions of 'Terrorism'

	Element	*Frequency*
1	Violence, force	83.5
2	Political	65
3	Fear, terror emphasized	51
4	Threat	47
5	Psychological effects and (anticipated) reactions	41.5
6	Victim-target differentiation	37.5
7	Purposive, planned, systematic, organized action	32
8	Method of combat, strategy, tactic	30.5
9	Extranormality, in breach of accepted rules, without humanitarian constraints	30
10	Coercion, extortion, induction of compliance	28
11	Publicity aspect	21.5
12	Arbitrariness; impersonal, random character; indiscrimination	21
13	Civilians, noncombatants, neutrals, outsiders as victims	17.5
14	Intimidation	17
15	Innocence of victims emphasized	15.5
16	Group, movement, organization as perpetrator	14
17	Symbolic aspect, demonstration to others	13.5
18	Incalculability, unpredictability, unexpectedness of occurrence of violence	9
19	Clandestine, covert nature	9
20	Repetitiveness; serial or campaign character of violence Criminal	7
21	Criminal	6
22	Demands made on third parties	4

Source: Alex P. Schmid, Albert J. Jongman et al., *Political Terrorism: A New Guide to Actors, Authors, Conepts, Data Bases, Theories, and Literature.* New Brunswick, Transaction Books, 1988, pp. 5-6

message' (political or otherwise) through his act of violence beyond facilitating the rapid handing over of his 'loot'.

The terrorist is also very different from the lunatic assassin, who may use identical tactics (e.g. shooting, bombing) and perhaps even seeks the same objective (e.g. the death of a political figure). However, while the tactics and targets of terrorists and lone assassins are often identical, their purpose is not. Whereas the terrorist's goal is again ineluctably *political* (to change or fundamentally alter a political system thought his violent act), the lunatic assassin's goal is more often intrinsically idiosyncratic, completely egocentric and deeply personal John Hinckley, who tried to kill President Reagan in 1981 to impress the actress Jodie Foster, is a case in point. He acted not from political motivation or ideological conviction but to fulfil some profound personal quest (killing the president to impress his screen idol). Such entirely *apoliticial* motivations can in no way be compared to the rationalizations used by the Narodnaya Volya to justify its campaign of tyrannicide against the tsar and his minions, nor even to the Irish Republican Army's efforts to assassinate Prime Minister Margaret Thatcher or her successor, John Major, in hopes of dramatically changing British policy towards Northern Ireland. Further, just as one person cannot credibly claim to be a political party, so a lone individual cannot be considered to constitute a terrorist group. In this respect, even though Sirhan Sirhan's assassination of presidential candidate and US Senator Robert Kennedy in 1968 had a political motive (to protest against US support for Israel), it is debatable whether the murder should be defined as a terrorist act since Sirhan belonged to no organized political group and acted entirely on his own,.out of deep personal frustration and a profound animus that few others shared.

By distinguishing terrorists from other types of criminals and terrorism from other forms of crime, we come to conclusion that terrorism is

- ineluctably political in aims and motives;
- violent - or, equally important, threatens violence;
- designed to have far-reaching psychological repercussions beyond the immediate victim or target;
- conducted by an organization with an identifiable chain of command or conspiratorial cell structure (whose members wear no uniform or identifying insignia); and
- perpetrated by a subnational group or no-state entity.

As such 'terrorism' is the deliberate creation and exploitation of fear through violence or the threat of violence in the pursuit of political change. All terrorist acts involve violence or the threat of violence. Terrorism is specifically designed to have far-reaching psychological effects beyond the immediate victim's or object of the terrorist attack. It is meant to instil fear within, and thereby intimidate, a wider 'target audience' that might include a rival ethnic or religious group, an entire country, a national government or political party, or public opinion in general. Terrorism is designed to create power where there is none or to consolidate power where there is very little.

7

Revolutionary Terrorism

In the days of British imperialism, many colonies opted the Revolutionary path for freedom of their countries from the clutches of oppressors. Not a police state such as the Soviet Union, Chile, Brazil, Uganda, or Cambodia, the society described here is the United States. The quotation is from *Prairie Fire* ("A single spark can start a prairie fire"), the revolutionary document of the Weather Underground. Date May 9, 1974, it is signed by the four founders of Weather Underground—Bernadine Dohrn, Billy Ayres, Jeff Jones, and Celia Sojourn.

These four young people do not urge a program of public education to reform the nation or advocate a drive for political action. They are not forming a new political party, lobbying in Washington on behalf of new legislation that might be progressive, or making speeches and printing books denouncing the shortcomings in the American society and suggesting reforms.

The Weather Underground urges armed conflict to destroy the political, economic, and social institutions of the United States. They claim credit for several bombings, including the Capital, State Department, and Pentagon in Washington.

The Weather Underground is obscene. It is so considered by most of the world's revolutionaries. Its criticisms of the quality of life in the United States are drenched in exaggeration and rhetoric, yet many Americans will agree with the criticisms. It is not at all difficult to find Americans who suggest that we imbibe too many alcoholic beverages or neglect our elder citizens. There are cases of children being beaten to death by frustrated and deranged parents. There are people in the United States, many of them, who do not get enough to eat. We are often more enamored with material objects than with that which ennobles a person. These and many more important criticisms are made constantly in the United States, from pulpits, in the halls of Congress, on the editorial pages and letters to the editors of newspapers. Library shelves are full of books devoted to them. Television editorials, specials, talk shows, and newscasts resound with these and many worse diatribes. In our homes and in the bars, where our culture "drinks itself to death," our faults and excesses are denounced.

All of these critics are not underground, but aboveground. They are real, live people. They sign their names. They urge and advocate reform. They give at least some of their time and energy toward improving the United States. In short, millions of Americans are trying in one way or another to do something constructive about themselves and their society. They are not issuing revolutionary manifestos. They are not advocating the blowing up of their country of trying to dynamite it into improvement. They do not endanger innocent people. They are not terrorists.

Again, the Weather Underground is obscene. To practice revolutionary terrorism in a land which affords ample protections for civil liberties and manifold opportunities for free speech and reformist actions is to impose a despotism worthy of Hitler and Stalin. Bernadine Dohrn, Billy Ayeers, Jeff Jones, and Celia Sojourn want not reform, not humanity, not political and economic equality, not any type of improved quality of life. They want *personal, destructive, self-aggrandizing, and quite cowardly power over other human beings.*

The same statement cannot be made about other revolutionary terrorists. Indeed, they suggest a moral quandary for the world. Suppose you lived in a land – you can pick any of a score or more in existence at the moment – ruled by a military dictatorship. All civil liberties have been cancelled. Justice has disappeared. You, your family, everyone you know is economically downtrodden. The wealth of the nation goes to the personal enrichment of the privileged few. Every day of your life you live under police rule. You live in terror of being arrested, tortured, and killed. You are powerless. Nowhere in the world is there anyone to help you or intervene on your behalf. You and others like you cannot vote the tyrants out of office. You do not have weapons to launch a civil war. Would you – indeed, should you – in this situation of gross oppression engage in terrorism as an act of revolution?

Certain it is that an affirmative answer has been given frequently throughout history. Human slavery, as practiced in the United Sates, was the most oppressive the world has ever know. Again and again slaves fought it. They ran away, they did poor work, they sabotaged the machinery and crops of their masters. There were several risings, the most famous of which was Nat Turner's Rebellion i 1831. Beginning with himself and six others, Turner set out at 10 P.M. on August 21 to free the slaves by murdering the slaveholders and their families. He marched from plantation to plantation in Virginia, sparing no one who owned slaves. Within hours his army had grown to seventy-five slaves. They left in their wake fifty-nine slain whites – men, women, and even infants.

To the white people of the South, Turner's was an act of sheer terror, invading sleeping plantations to murder innocent people in their beds. The whites summoned the most repressive measures to capture and hang Turner and his men and to prevent such an insurrection from ever happening again. To black Americans, Turner is to this day a hero, a courageous man fighting for freedom. Who is correct?

The long, bloody history of labor violence in the United States was studded with acts of terrorism. Union men felt driven to it because all other resources were closed to them until the 1930's. Their unions, their strikes were illegal. Virtually all powers of the law were arrayed against them. During strikes they were confronted with the overwhelming power of company police, strikebreakers, local police, national guardsmen, and even federal troops. In such situations they repeatedly resorted to terrorism. They bombed and gunned down company officers.

Perhaps the most colorful episode of union terrorism were the Molly Maguires in the anthracite coal fields of Pennsylvania in the 1860's and 1870's. The miners worked waist deep in water, amid appalling safety conditions, for starvation wages. Their unions and their strikes for better wages and working conditions were consistently overpowered. The miners, all native to Ireland, organized a secret society dubbed the Molly Maguires. For over fifteen years they fought the mine owners with terror. Mine officials were murdered and others scared away by threats. The power of the Molly Maguires was eventually broken when their organization was infiltrated by a Pinkerton detective. The leaders were arrested, and several were executed. Did their activities constitute terrorism or blows for freedom and economic justice?

Nazi Germany under Adolf Hitler practiced perhaps the most despotic form of *state terrorism* in modern times. From 1938 to 1945, most of the peoples of Western and Eastern Europe were subjugated one after the other by German arms. People were murdered by the millions. For the captive people, all political freedom was lost. They lived amid economic deprivation and finally near starvation. They were forced to work under conditions that amounted to slave labor.

The captive people maintained an underground resistance. Men and women, secretly armed by allied forces, sabotaged German troop trains, destroyed bridges, and killed Germans whenever they could. To Americans and British, these resistance forces were heroes, courageous Dutch or Danes or French fighting for freedom. To the Germans they were terrorists, and they sought to stamp them out with the most savage repression and reprisals. Who was right?

In the late 1950's, the people of Hungary rebelled against Soviet rule, then were overpowered by Soviet tanks and soldiers. We called the Hungarians who warred against such odds freedom fighters. The Soviets thought them terrorist revolutionaries. Who was right?

To repeat the words of Henry B. Burnett, Jr., editor of *Skeptic* magazine: "Your terrorist is my patriot."

State terrorism breeds revolutionary terrorism, and the more repressive the government, the more desperate the terrorism. The situation in Brazil provides an example. Marico Moreira Alves, in the article previously quoted, describes the situation this way:

> The outside world is not told that an increasing concentration of wealth limits to a shrinking few the profits from industrial expansion. No mention is made of the hunger and misery that drive millions of landless peasants to the cities. Most important of all, the foreign press fails to expose the incredible violence that the state itself must use to keep the masses quiet while the privileged squander the nation's riches.

The situation described by Alves is chaotic. Most of the burgeoning industry is foreign owned and supported by the military regime in Brazil. The high profits are derived from the labor of underpaid workers. Trade unionism has all but disappeared. The millions of unemployed, crowded into urban shantytowns called *favelas,* are used by the system as a reserve army of jobless so that those who have jobs work for low wages. Alves feels that revolution is the only solution to Brazil's problem—and that terrorism is the only means of carrying out the revolution. "When all the established paths to change are barred," he writes, "only the road of revolution remains open ... The revolutionary movement in Brazil has developed a set of original tactics—those of the urban guerrilla."

The aim of the urban guerrilla. as Alves puts its, is "of demoralizing the repressive system and of creating economic difficulties." It is harassment. Why urban? Because that is where most of the people are. There, it is easier to harass, then to hide among the masses of the people. It is hit-and-run warfare conducted no in the mountains or countryside where guerrilla warfare began, but in the cities where life is most fragile and people are most vulnerable.

The majority of the people of Rhodesia and the Union of South Africa are blacks yet they are among the most oppressed people on earth. They are economically impoverished, living in squalor. They are denied virtually all political activity and the most basic human rights. They are subjected to the most despotic social, economic, and political segregation under the apartheid policies of the white South African government. The situation has been called a ticking time bomb for South Africa and the world, for the blacks of that attractive land are determined to govern their country, win their freedom, and end their oppression. They are rioting, fighting, and terrorizing for these purposes.

The situations in Brazil and South Africa are similar to situations in half a hundred or more nations with oppressive, militaristic governments. Some are Communist. Others are anticommunist. Not a few are fascist. All are totalitarian police states.

How do we as Americans feel about these situations? Our ancestors fired the shot "heard round the world." In the Declaration of Independence and the Constitution we proclaim the virtues of life, liberty, the pursuit of happiness, and the joys of self-government. The shot is still being heard. Oppressed people all over the world know and want what we Americans consider a birthright and often take for granted. Chances are most Americans respect and admire and feel sympathy for people who fight for their liberty.

The central question remains: is terrorism an acceptable a part of that revolutionary struggle for liberty? Historically, revolutions have involved a certain amount of terrorism. Police and government officials, sometimes even rulers were shot. There were bombings and riots. The revolution occurred when the rulers lost the ability to govern effectively, and new rulers came in either with the support of the people or with enough military power to force their will on the people.

Americans should not forget that the model for many revolutions, particularly those of the left, was the American Revolution. The techniques of revolution developed by Samuel Adams of Boston have been copied successfully scores of times since 1776. The method involves the formation of secret underground organizations – in Adams' case the so-called Caucus clubs, which are thought to have planned many of Boston's street disorders, such as the Stamp Act riots, the tarring and feathering of those who defied non-importation agreements, the public ruckus that brought on the Boston Massacre. Incidents like the latter are then propagandized into major instances of oppression so as to inflame a significant portion of the population into revolution. Most revolutions, except for the right-wing military dictatorships, begin in quite similar fashion.

If the oppression is great and the need for revolution paramount, then perhaps terrorism is justified—or so it seems to a militant minority living in conditions they believe oppressive. What form of terrorism? Blowing up a prison containing a torture chamber? Slaying the head of the secret police? Assassinating the head of the government? But these methods are both difficult to accomplish and not very effective. Another person with a better torture chamber can always be built. A new chief of police will be named, and another colonel or commissar, perhaps worse, will take charge of the government.

The *aim of any revolution is to bring down the government and replace it with one of a different type.* This may also involve replacing the economic system and many of the social institutions. But when the government is powerful and very oppressive, this is a most difficult task. One of the aims of torture and state terrorism is to intimidate and neutralize the majority of the people, so the government can concentrate on the militant minority ready to die for the cause. The government is then able to bring all its police power to bear on the revolu-tionaries. It is extremely difficult for a revolution to succeed in this situation. Too much power is arrayed against it.

The revolutionary terrorists, faced with such obstacles, have a powerful motive for extending their violence to other targets—innocent people. Unable to make much headway against their real oppressors, there is a temptation to bomb an embassy, shoot a diplomat, kidnap a foreign businessman, skyjack a plane. Or worse: shoot up a foreign airport, bomb a bank in New York or London that lends money to their country, or any of a dozen other infamous acts. For the Iranian terrorists, it was a simple matter to declare the Shah of Iran an "American puppet" and then shoot two Americans who happened to be in the country. There have been scores of similar incidents. The ramifications of such actions are merely appalling.

Why would terrorists, seeking to end oppression in their own country, bomb and shoot innocent people in other countries? There is a certain perverse logic to such actions that we need to understand. Killing an American because oppression exists in Iran or Brazil or South Africa or India or any of a score of other places offers what the revolutionary terrorists consider distinct advantages.

The first is publicity. The crime, particularly if it is brutal and ghastly—even better if it can be long drawn out as in a skyjacking—becomes a "media event." The world's press, radio, and television center on the terrorism—for an hour, a day, a week. The demands of the terrorists are reported. They have their moment in the spotlight. The world has suddenly heard of them. And that is important, for most people are unaware of oppression in countries such as Brazil or Chile.

Some people are dismayed at the killing and maiming of innocent people. But others, trying to foment their own revolutions or having only recently won a successful one, are sympathetic. The terrorists earn respect, moral support, aid in the form of money, weapons and tactical advice. They could have shot at the local police for years and not accomplished a fraction of what a single bomb in New York or an attack on airlines accomplished in minutes.

International terrorist attacks on innocents has other advantages for the revolution. The violent acts are cited as "proof" that the terrorists are desperate, willing to risk all for the cause, even their lives. It proves they are strong enough and well organized enough to hijack the airplane or bomb the embassy or whatever. The terrorism supposedly makes the revolutionary movement a viable organization, able to lead and to act. It is supposed to help rally the oppressed and dissatisfied people under the banner of the terrorist organization.

Acts of international terrorism are also supposed to have the advantage of increasing the "righting spirit" of the revolutionaries and of toughening the people for the revolutionary struggle.

The need for terrorist acts to achieve publicity can be reduced by consistent reporting of the oppression that exists in the world. The work of Amnesty International is terribly important in this regard. The organization calls attention to the torture and state terrorism that exists in the world. Through this publicity, the organization seeks to rally world opinion against the oppressive regime and negotiate an end to the torture. Much of the free world's press has reported the findings of Amnesty International. Other newsmen have reported oppression on their own. All such activities should be increased, for they defuse terrorism by removing the need for publicity. If the world already knows and disapproves of the oppression in Chile or South Africa, the revolutionaries will have less need to blow up innocent people to make their own cause known.

A related action is to have international sanctions imposed against oppressive regimes. This has happened in the case of Cuba, Rhodesia and South Africa. Congress has withdrawn aid from Turkey. The United States, because of its own revolution and its history of civil liberty and self-government, can be a moral force for condemning oppression. There have been many cases in which we have given foreign aid to totalitarian regimes simply because they were anticommunist. There has long been opposition to this practice among Americans, many of whom feel it is a tragic error. Greater American opposition to oppression wherever it exists would help to ease off the threat of revolutionary terrorism. In 1977, President Jimmy Carter began such an effort. He spoke out forcefully in defense of human rights and threatened economic sanctions against those nations that violate them.

Opposition to oppression is a two-way street, however, for misguided terrorism in the name of phony revolution is also despotic and oppressive. As was suggested earlier, any hoodlum can declare his crime an act of political terrorism. Such acts need to be clearly labeled "CRIME". Terrorism by lunatic minorities in countries such as the United States, which offer basic political freedoms and rule by law, should also be denounced and punished as crime.

The people of the world are not helpless, nor are they without perception. It is possible to tell the difference between real oppression and imaginary. It is possible to recognize real revolution and to denounce crime in the nature of revolution for personal gain. Both the real and the phony exist in the world. With a little information, it is not hard to tell the difference and to do something about both.

Four types of terrorism namely: criminal terrorism, terrorism for ethnic or national liberation, state terrorism and revolutionary terrorism are remarkable. The acts of terrorists may be the same, but it is important to understand that the motives and rationale are different. To lump all terrorism together is a tragic error, for actions that might be used against one type would be a mistake against another. Criminal terrorists, for example, might be hunted down by police, arrested, tried and sent to prison. To do the same against revolutionary terrorists means an extension of state terrorism and the worsening of the oppression, thus acting as a goad to further revolutionary terrorism. Conversely, if an effort is made to defuse genuine revolutionary terrorism by publicizing their just cause, this can encourage gangsterism by permitting simple crime to be masked by phony claims of oppression. So, need to consider which type of terrorism we are dealing with to take effective measures against it.

Then, there are all the problems associated with that much-abused word "liberation". We need to make a proper distinction between oppressed people who want political freedom, such as South Africans and others and extreme nationalists groups who want to "liberate" a piece of territory from "colonial" rule. We need to recognize that such groups as the Palestinians, the IRA, the Basques, the South Moluccans, the French-Canadian separatists and the Puerto Rican nationalists are not liberating anything, but oppressing the people of the world. Their claims are subject to peaceful solution—perhaps by negotiation, perhaps by majority rule, perhaps by greater local autonomy. Therefore, their terrorism make them oppressors, not liberators. So is the need to separate the real and the genuine from the imagined, rhetorical, spurious and feigned.

8

Terrorism As Crime

Who are terrorists? What do they want? Why do they hate so much? And what can be done to stop them? Psychiatrists, psychologists, scholars, and various other experts have been asked to "explain" the phenomenon of terrorism by answering these questions. Several views appear most frequently. One is that terrorism is not really very common. Far more people are killed in automobile accidents each year than are victims of terrorism. But this analogy does not apply. Traffic accidents are a personal tragedy, but they are still accidents, happenstance. They do not carry with them the horror and intimidation associated with a deliberate act of bombing, murder, or kidnapping.

The political gains can be more specific than that. The horrible massacres committed by various Palestinian terrorist groups have not been successful in their avowed aim of driving the Israelis out of the Holy Land. But they have had an immense political benefit to the Palestinians. The cause of Palestine liberation has received worldwide publicity. Arab nations have been forced to say there can be no settlement of the boundary and other disputes with Israel unless the "Palestine question" is also resolved. The leader of the Palestine Liberation Organization, Yasser Arafat, has addressed the United Nations General Assembly–wearing a gun. These are no small political gains from the random murder of innocent human beings.

Another way to explain *modern terrorism is as total war.* It is suggested that murdering and maiming civilians is not much different from the "terror bombings" of World War II and subsequent conflicts. In modern warfare both sides indiscriminately bomb the other's cities, hoping the terror will inhibit the ability and will of the people to carry on the war. Terrorists, who believe they are at war with society, a country, or a situation, are simply applying the same tactics.

Another view to this is that we are all our brother's keeper, that we are all guilty for any injustice that occurs in the world. This is certainly a concept widely advocated by the terrorists themselves. It has an obvious usefulness, as was pointed out by Dr. Hannah Arendt in her celebrated essay *On Violence:*

> Rage and violence turn irrational only when they are directed against substitutes ... It has become rather fashionable among white liberals to react to Negro grievances with the cry. "We are all guilty," and black Power has proved only too happy to take advantage of this "confession" to instigate an irrational "black rage." Where all are guilty, no one is: confessions of collective guilt are the best possible safeguard against the discovery of culprits.

Another still-related view traces the rise in terrorism to the "moral breakdown" in modern society. According to this thinking, terrorism and other forms of violence have risen along with permissiveness in society, gradual deterioration of the family, alienation, identity crises, sexual license, pornography, drunkenness, drug addiction, deterioration in the work ethic, and generalized thrill seeking.

The much observed "moral breakdown" - if there is one—doubtless is something of a factor in the rise of terrorism, but the simple fact is that there are millions of alienated, culturally deprived individuals, all products of a permissive society and devoid of traditional morality, who do not shoot innocent children in airports or decapitate innocent travelers with airport bombs.

Many attempts have been made to provide a psychiatric profile of the new terrorists. Dr. David G. Hubbard, psychiatrist and director of the Aberrant Behaviour Center in Dallas, studied forty-six skyjackers and their companions. He reported the typical skyjacker's father was often a violent alcoholic, his mother a religious fanatic. The skyjacker was ofter poorly coordinated as a child, earning ridicule for being clumsy. He did poorly in school and seldom date girls. He dreamed frequently about unaided flight, had difficulty holding a job, made a poor marriage and had few friends. He was sexually inadequate and possessed a subconscious wish to die.

One view comes from Edmond Taylor, writing in the summer 1973 issue of *Horizon,* in an article entitled "The terrorists." He reported that analysis of Kozo Okamoto, the twenty-four-year old Japanese terrorist captured following the Lod Airport massacre, had shown him to be prepared to die for something he vaguely described as "world revolution on behalf of the world proletarian." Taylor comments:

> He had demonstrated that he was ready to sacrifice himself in this ideologically ambiguous combat, but he probably would have been equally ready to die for a united Catholic Ireland, an independent Quebec, or possibly even for a peronist Argentina. Fanatical commitment to a revolutionary cause so vague that it is interchangeable with almost any other is one of the characteristic traits of the modern terrorist.

Another way to explain terrorism is in terms of hate-hatred so bitter, so all-consuming that the hater turns terrorist. Fawaz Turki, a young Palestinian, described his hatred in his book *The Disinherited:*

> And so I hated. I hated the world and the order or reality around me. I hated being dispossessed of a nation and an identity. I hated not being part of a culture. I hated being a hybrid, an outcast, a zero. A problem ...
>
> So I hated, and the world hated me because I hated.
>
> ... Give me a gun, man, and I will blow my own or somebody else's brain out.

Edmond Taylor , in the article quoted above, had another view of such hatred, however. He suggested that the hatred reflects a "keen sense of psychological strategy." In his opinion many of the more brutish acts of terrorism, such as the Lod raid, were "deliberately planned to produce the impression of irrational, almost maniacal violence." Taylor called this "the strategy of the absurd," a conscious effort to appear irrational and mad and therefore unpredictable, thereby unaffected by threats, persuasion, or bribes. He sees this strategy of the absurd, this use of the totally irrational act as "basic strategy" of world terrorism.

Then there is frustration as a cause for terrorism. Dr. Abrahamsen addressed himself to this in *U.S. News & World Report (1974):*

> They are exceedingly frustrated ... They see no chance to achieve their goals peacefully, of persuading a large number of ordinary people to accept their vision. Since they are frustrated, they take their revenge against the establishment, hoping to dramatize their vision and their power.

Most of these expert opinions, and many others that might be cited, surely have value. But the sheer variety of these opinions indicates the chief value may be in indicating what a complex problem modern terrorism is.

In moving closer to understanding the problem of terrorism if we realize that it is incorrect to lump all terrorists together. Drawing profiles of *the* terrorist and explaining his or her motives is probably a futile exercise. It may have value in explaining one or ever all the Palestinian terrorists, but it will miss the mark in explaining a Tupamaro in Uruguay or a victim of apartheid in South Africa.

There are four distinct types of terrorism in the world:

- criminal terrorism
- terrorism for ethnic or national liberation
- state terrorism
- revolutionary terrorism.

Each has different purpose, motive, rationale, and tactics. To link them together is a mistake. Each problem must be treated separately so it can be combated in a different manner. There is one solution to all terrorism. And our world wide efforts are hampered by our failure to recognize these four distinct types. The Americans are most familiar with criminal terrorism–individuals, gangs, or criminal organizations preying on people for personal gain. They see it almost daily: people afraid to go out after dark (sometimes even in daylight) for fear of being mugged; street gangs fighting each other or breaking up public events such as occurred at Detroit's Cobo Hall in 1976; people being gunned down on the street for no rational reason, except that the gunman wants to prove he or she could do it; gangs invading homes or business, intimidating and even killing people as hostages; organized rackets threatening storekeepers unless they pay for "protection."

When the group led by Charles Manson went on a crime rampage in Los Angeles in 1969, killing nine people, including movie actress Sharon Tate, it was suggested that his killing were part of some vague plot to overthrow the government. Most people dismissed this, seeing the murders as what they were–unspeakable crimes by deranged people. Nonetheless, the remnants of Manson's "family" are still listed among "revolutionary" organizations in the United Sates.

When the Symbionese Liberation Army, having made Patricia Hearst either a captive or a convert to their beliefs, went on a spree of robbing banks and shooting up stores, this was advertised as a blow for freedom. Yet, robbing banks and shooting up stores is rather conventional criminal activity. Even among terrorist groups, the activities of Symbionese Liberation Army were highly suspect. Certain it is that the money obtained in the robberies hardly went toward even a misguided effort to "liberate" anyone. Indeed, Desmond Smith, suggested, the SLA was very clever in "ransoming" Patricia Hearst with a huge giveaway of food to the poor in the city of Oakland, California. Its purpose was to "neutralize the normal public response" to the crime of kidnapping and "cloak crime with a veneer of respectability." (*The Nation,* 1974).

There is considerable suspicion that at least some of the kidnappings now routinely performed throughout the world are motivated more by personal gain than by conceptions of fighting for freedom. As much as $55 million has been paid to free kidnap victims. Several payments of more than a million dollars have been made. Supposedly the money goes to buy guns and explosives to further carry on terrorist activities. But again, it seems to be easy to commit a crime, then state it was done by a terrorist organization as an act of political liberation. Too many kidnappings and murders and robberies have been committed by "terrorist organizations" which no one ever heard of before or after the crime.

The line between crime and political terrorism becomes exceedingly precise. The weapons are often similar. The acts of kidnapping, murder, and robbery are the same. The hijacking of commercial airlines, long favored by terrorists, began as a criminal act for gain in which the plane, its passengers, and crew were held for ransom by a gunman.

In the end, perhaps only personal motivation differentiates the terrorist from the criminal, and that line sometimes becomes very fuzzy.

For almost ten years. Northern Ireland has been the scene of mayhem. More than sixteen hundred people have been killed and tens of millions of dollars worth of property damaged. Ostensibly, it is a battle between Catholics and Protestants for political and economic control of the six northern countries. The dominant Protestant majority wants to remain part of the United Kingdom. The Catholics, or many of them, want unification with the Republic of Ireland. The cutting edges of this bloodshed are Protestant paramilitary groups and the Irish Republican Army. They bomb and shoot each other regularly. Yet, there have been many crimes that make no sense. They accomplish nothing for either side and may even be self-defeating. It is now widely believed by both sides that the ideological conflict for control of the north is being used in many instances to mask simple crime. It is believed by both Catholics and Protestants that at least some of the murders have been personal vendettas or killings by savage lunatics for the simple joy of killing. A Belfast psychiatrist has observed a sharp drop in the number of psychopaths admitted to local hospitals. They are out in the streets committing mayhem.

The three members of the Japanese Red Army who perpetrated the Lod Airport massacre wanted to die. One is believed to have committed suicide with a hand grenade. Kozo Okamoto, who was captured, is reportedly bitter that the Israelis will not execute him. Such suicidal tendencies are often symptomatic of mental illness. This view is enhanced by the fact the Japanese Red Army is known to have tortured and killed with ice picks fourteen of its own members for "unrevolutionary behaviour." Okamoto's concept of world revolution is so vague as hardly to qualify as an ideology. And the Japanese hired out as mercenary "hit men" of the most grotesque sort. It all smacks more of simple crime than political terrorism. It should be labeled as such and dealt with as such. The world has had much more experience dealing with crime than with political terrorism.

There have been several terrorist gangs whose espousal of political causes is highly suspect as mere lip service. Perhaps the most infamous was the Baader-Meinhof gang in Germany. It created a gory trail of bombings, bank robberies, and shoot-outs before most of its members were captured in 1972. The list of charges against arsonist Andreas Baader and Ulrike Meinhof and others included five counts of murder and fifty-four of attempted murder.

Ulrike Meinhof committed suicide in her cell in Germany in 1976. Forty-one years old, she was the daughter of a museum director and had once been a prominent left-wing journalist. She had also worked with delinquent girls until she persuaded herself to teach them to take up arms against a society that defined them as deliquents. Psychiatrists who examined this so-called revolutionary described her behavior as "unbalanced sexual jealousy." The gang members were fascinated by the powerful Mercedes-benzes and Porsches they stole and used in their raids. They wore pistols at the ready. Ulrike Meinhof had been married to a rich and influential left-wing publisher. It is theorized that she drifted into terror out of boredom and lack of direction. What resulted in bombings of empty buildings spread to murder and shoot-outs with police.

Andreas Baader and Ulrike Meinhof resemble the Americans Bonnie and Clyde, a shabby pair of bank robbers of the 1930's. To publicize and thereby honor their vague political mutterings about oppression and liberation is to lend a cast of altruism and respectability to criminals.

There have been many such criminal gangs masquerading as political reformers, including the ten-members Angry Brigade in Britain, all sentenced to ten years in prison for their crimes. Another is a "guerrilla group" formed in Argentina by Angel Bengochea. His group had neither name nor ideology, but he and four followers went ahead anyhow. They rented a luxury apartment and filled it with guns, bazookas, hand grenades, rockets, and dynamite. The whole collection exploded, bringing the entire seven-story building down with it and killing Bengochea and his followers. Nonetheless, publicity was given to bengochea's obituary addressed to his wife. "I know we cannot achieve a just society unless we achieve what is human by inhuman ways." Not only is the logic of the statement ridiculous, but so is permitting a man who is either deranged or a criminal to cloak himself in high purpose.

There is terrorism that is politically motivated lots of it, but there is also crime and lots of that, too. It does not take much cleverness to dream up some vague "revolution" or "injustice" to justify a robbery or murder as a "blow for freedom" for the "oppressed" people of the world. It is not much of an exaggeration, if any, to foresee the day when every street mugger, pickpocket, and pimp will be mouthing political slogans to gain sympathy for his crimes.

9

Management of Terrorist Organizations

This chapter intends to answer three questions: What is the main characteristic of terrorist organizations that affects their infrastructure? What does the infrastructure look like? How does this infrastructure affect the behavior of terrorists. On the analystical level of group dynamics? Infrastructure in this context means an internal organizational structure, including formal and informal networks within that structure. It is this thesis that this structure affects the behaviour and activities of terrorists. The data comes from nonclassified, open sources in five languages dealing with active terrorist movements in the United Sates and abroad, as of 1980. Since it is impossible, for security reasons, to acquire reliable information from first-hand interviews with terrorists, this chapter relies on scattered data which in many instances defies verification. Nonetheless, for someone like this writer, who had five years of combat service as an urban guerrilla during World War II, the data provides a sufficient basis for conclusions to be drawn from uniformly present characteristics across several cultures.

Main Characteristic of Terrorist Organizations

The relatively small size of the group is the primary characteristic of a terrorist organization. By contrast, the European underground movements, so well developed during World War II and so efficient in their systematic terrorist activities, were according to any standards huge organizations. For example, the Polish Underground Movement (*Armia Krajowa*) in 1944 had over 380,000 front-line troops plus at least an equal number of support members, totaling 760,000 people. The membership of the Italian Resistance was somewhere between 150,000-200,000; the French Forces of the Interior (FFI) for the northern and southern zones, about 425,000. Both effective management of the flow of communications up and down the chain of command and maintenance of the security for such masses of those involved demanded establishment of a rigid, hierarchial organizational structure patterned on military models. The smallest unit was a section of three to six persons; the members knew each other only by pseudonyms. In addition to his men, the leader of a section knew only four to six other section leaders of his platoon and his officer or a cadet, knew the section leaders of his platoon, the other platoon commanders, and his company commander. The company commander, usually a second or first lieutenant, knew only his platoon leaders, other company commanders, and his battalion commnader, and so on up the ladder. Limiting the contacts and the circle within which each person interacted provided maximum security for those involved. However, this system made the process of communication slow. For an order from central headquarters to reach a private in a section, had to descend through each level of the organization. In an urban setting, it took at least two to three days for an order from the commander in chief to reach a private in a section; an example was the order for mobilization to start the Uprising of Warsaw in 1944. This hierarchical organizational framework, cumbersome as it was, seemed the best under the circumstances when members numbered hundreds of thousands.

In the United Sates, twelve to sixteen groups presently aspire to revolutionary change violent means membership in each of them does not exceed forty to fifty people.

The Red Brigades in Italy are estimated by their own membership to number from four hundred to ten thousand, depending on who is counting and whether the sympathizers, who do not handle weapons, are also included. The Badder-Meinhof Gang was composed of approximately one hundred members. The Japanese Red Army fluctuates between thirty and forty members; the Palestinian group El Ansar, less than two hundred; Action Organization for the Liberation of Palestine, less than three hundred.

The Infrastructure

A division of labour takes place among terrorists and some structure is needed to channel communication and to coordinate activities. The small size of these groups imposes on them an infrastructure quite different from those of underground movements during World War II.

The centrifugal terrorist infrastructure resembles that of a solar system: the leader is the sun, and the members are surrounding planets, usually within the range of his direct impact. Thus, in the hierarchial system, the leader is at the top; in the centrifugal system, the leader is, so to speak, in the center. This arrangement has great consequences on the behavior of terrorists.

Impact of Infrastructure on Behaviour of Terrorists

Eleven patterns which are the direct results of centrifugal infrastructures are submitted here: ten are distinctly different from the behaviour of hierarchical organizations, and one points to similarity.

1) The leaders of terrorist movements, by virtue of being in the center of their organizations, not only act as direct catalysts of actions, by planning and giving orders, but they are also participants in the actions. This arrangement is extremely important to the rank and file. Such an organizational structure provides the

leaders with a high degree of visibility. They suffer equally with their fellow members all the consequences of action, including wounds and death. They share psychological stress beforehand and periods of decompression after action, with all its misery, floating anxieties, and tensions. These kinds of shared experiences build more intensely personalized loyalties than are characteristic in hierarchical organizations.

2) The centrifugal system secures more direct and rapid communication. This increases flexibility of action and success in combat operations, by allowing the leader himself to reassess the feasibility of an action on the basis of new and personally ascertained information. Moreover, it removes a common anxiety-producing dilemma among low-ranking leaders of a hierarchical organization: being required to execute a plan that has been rendered unfeasible due to changed circumstances. Under these conditions, such leaders, as a rule, go ahead with the action, fearful of charges of disobeying orders, or of what to them is a worse punishment, criticism and ostracism by their peers.

3) Direct accessibility to the leader enables him to tap and react immediately to the most ingenious schemes conceived and the location of targets reported by rank and file. This further enhances tactical flexibility and allows terrorist groups to operate against targets of opportunity, a factor that is particularly important given the asymmetrical power relationship existing between the terrorists and the government they are attacking.

4) Another important feature of the centrifugal infrastructure is its independence from society's support. The hierarcical organization, by virtue of its very size and complexity, cannot exist without extensive social support. Moreover, it takes one to two years to develop such a complex network. By contrast, the centrifugal system is so small that it can exist independently of

support networks; it is so mobile that it can be relocated quickly. But, above all, it can be created and mobilized instantaneously. Such a system has no files, no records, and no bureaucracy hindering its activities. An organization so independent of society that it has no fear of society's response presents a dangerous situation—the terrorists operate under no constraints.

In the case of hierarchical organization, public opinion can hinder recruitment, thus causing its collapse. In a centrifugal system, the leader does not need public sentiment to provide adherents; he need only the loyalty of his immediate followers. Even progressive annihilation of the immediate environment will not affect the physical integrity of a centrifugal unit–it will move to another area. During the five years of World War II, Polish society daily lost an average of three thousand people, killed by the Germans occupying central and western Poland. Eastern Poland was occupied by the Soviet army from September 1939 until the outbreak of war between Germany and the Soviet Union in June 1941. This blood-letting had an immense effect on the structure of the Polish Underground. Under these circumstances, centrifugal organizations would remain relatively unaffected.

5) Direct access to the leader by the rank and file allows the latter to identify with the power of mythical and magical qualities usually attributed to the former and, as such, enables the followers to participate in his charisma. The father-figure image, so eagerly instilled by leaders among members, is reinforced; during Castro's early revolutionary activity, his Cuban followers sang a ditty: "Eisenhower, ha, ha, ha, Fidel Castro your papa!" Moreover, leaders have the opportunity to give direct moral dispensation for deeds which might otherwise be repudiated by certain standards of society or by the early upbringing of members. All these factors

are helpful in freeing the members of internal dilemmas and in giving them self-images of heroes with a unity of purpose.

6) The leader also is directly involved in the selection and recruitment of new members to the group. The leader's personal role in recruitment is usually so magnetic and ego-gratifying to incoming members that such recruitment to the centrifugal organization is not related to the prospects of success of the organization. There too is some evidence that motivation behind joining a centrifugal organization is much less related to perception of threat than was the case with underground organization in World War II.

7) Centrifugal groups tend to seek cooperation and allies not with stronger groups, but with those whom they can easily manipulate. Consequently, they coalesce on the peer level and are extremely wary of any involvements which may be powerful enough to impose demands on them and thus curb freedom of their activities. The major powers have perceived this tendency and have assisted terrorists indirectly, through smaller states: e.g., Czechoslovakia, North Korea, Cuba, Bulgaria, East Germany, Hungary, Iraq, and Syria. The countries of Algeria, Yemen, Libya, Uganda, Saudi Arabia, and Cyprus also have been involved in assisting and, in many instances, providing cover for the major or original sources of support.

This inclination of centrifugal terrorist organizations to ally with their peers has led to the development of informal networks and has led to the development of informal networks and has influenced both training and operations. Both German and Japanese terrorists have received training in camps run by various Palestinian groups, and several leaders of Italy's Red Brigades were trained in Czechoslovakia. In one of the best known terrorist episodes, three members of the Japanese Red Army attacked Lod Airport outside Tel Aviv in 1972 on behalf of the Palestinians, one faction of which–the Popular Front for the Liberation of Palestine–had provided them their training in Lebanon, Members of the Baader-Meinhof Gang helped hijack a French airlines bound for Israel and forced it to fly to Entebbe. Police have also established links between the Baader-Meinhof Gang and the Venezuelan terrorist "Carlos," the Red Brigades, and the Japanese Red Army.

In 1974, several representatives from terrorist organizations, including Basques, Irish, Croatians, Bretons, Welsh, and Catalans, gathered to discuss their mutual needs. Also in 1974, representatives of terrorists groups from Uruguay, Bolivia, and Chile met in Buenos Aires to establish a junta for revolutionary coordination Paraguayans, Dominicans, Colombians, and Venezuelans joined the junta. Mutual exchanges of trained personnel, weapons, and money followed. According to at least one source, it is reported that Libya, Iraq, and South Yemen provide money, weapons and sanctuary for terrorist groups.

8) Comparing the centrifugal vis-a-vis hierarchical extralegal violent organizations, it is attempted here also to ascertain to what degree the members of the centrifugal organization are able to maintain their anonymity. Presumably, this should be difficult in view of their direct accessibility to the leader. Anonymity is an important determining factor of terrorist behavior, because the less identity a terrorist has within the group, the less he feels personally responsible toward outsiders for the actions of the group. However, it was not possible to find sufficiently reliable data to submit to the reader any sound generalization.

9) There seems to be in all types of human organizations the need for the establishment of a working network within which, in time, a certain bureaucratic "bloat" takes place. Comparative studies of French, Italian, Polish, Soviet, and Vietnamese hierarchical clandestine

organizations indicate over time the presence in their structures of these two bureaucratic phenomena: an increase in numbers of bureaucrats in excess of actual need; and the Peter Principle, or movement upward on the administrative ladder to the point where on reaches on's maximum level of incompetence.

This phenomenon is particularly true in hierarchical organizations. After World War II, the bureaucracy of the British Admiralty grew from 2000 to 3569 officials, while the Royal Navy's uniformed manpower decreased by one third and the number of ships in commission decreased by two thirds. A New York Department study in 1974 indicated that the force had grown by 55 per cent over twenty years, but the number of policemen on the beat or cruising in cars remained the same. In 1974, the Italian Navy had more admirals than ships and one general for five thousand troops. In the same year, a French general or admiral commanded an average of seventeen hundred men. Hierarchical clandestine organizations also are subject to considerable bloating, with a proliferation of secretaries, messengers, and bodyguards. There is no bloating in centrifugal organizations for two reason: such bloating would hamper the leader's direct exercise of power, and the small size of the organization mitigates against it. The result is enhanced efficiency.

10) The leader's direct control over membership is tremendously enhanced in centrifugal organizations. During World War II, the commander of the Resistance in Milan, when asked about the membership of his units and his control over them, said: "Six hundred if things are difficult, six thousand if things are not so difficult, and of course sixty thousand if things are easy." This is not the case within the centrifugal system; here, members are within the direct range of the leader's vision. Control is exercised speedily and without mercy. As a result, it

is much easier to join a terrorist organization than to withdraw from it.

11) Finally, one important similarity between hierarchical and centrifugal organizations should be mentioned. When either type of organization is threatened by stresses from within, their respective leaders will use external violence as a means of keeping the membership together. In other words, internal problems of the organization ofter serve as catalysts of external violence. There are examples of this phenomenon, but, for understandable reasons, they are very difficult to prove and never officially admitted. Many actions have been ordered when there was no tactical, strategic, or political reasons for using violence, except to fulfill the need perceived by a leader: either to distract the membership from internal problems, to restore cohesion, or for the leader's personal reasons, known only to him. These actions are always carried out under the label of a great cause.

Considering these eleven behavioral characteristics of contemporary terrorist organizations that are directly related to their infrastructure, what can we infer about trends for the future? First of all, according to statistics, the curve of frequency of world-wide attacks defies prognosis.

It is safe to assume that many more incidents were not reported. During the same period, the total number of people killed by terrorists was 2, 102; The wounded numbered 5,078. On the other hand, figures for the United States and Canada for the period 1975-78 show a steady decrease in the number of terrorist incidents. It is not necessarily correct, however, to conclude that the diminishing frequency of terrorist activities in this country has decreased the threat of terrorism to society. In fact, as much, if not more, harm is resulting from greater selectivity and sensitivity in choosing objects of attack.

It might be useful to readers to take a closer look at the domestic situation. By any criteria, we Americans live in an extremely violent culture. In 1978, there was one murder every 27 minutes. In the same year, one million violent acts were committed. We are subjected daily to violence in the media. In 1973, 70 per cent of programs on television depicted acts of violence. By the time an average American youngster reaches his eighteenth birthday, he will have witnessed 18 thousand murders of television. Undoubtedly, this has some effect on our capacity to accept violence as a problem-solving mechanism, and sensitivities toward the sanctity of human life are dulled by such exposures. The rate of homicides has been climbing consistently since 1963. The sex of the perpetrators of violence also reflects cultural values—four out of five homicides and nine out ten robberies in the United States are committed by males, although the rate of increase in female participation in violent acts is increasing more rapidly than that for men.

The large number of illegal aliens in the United States also is relevant as a potential source of violence. Estimated to be between 6 and 12 million, they come from fifty-one nations. Their illegal entry into this country makes them vulnerable to police harassment and provides fertile ground for illegal organized violence. Some scientists speculate that the perception of threat can easily induce human beings to violent aggressive behaviour.

Thus, the question is raised: in light of the high visibility of violence and the potential for violence in the United Sates, why do we have so relatively few and small terrorist groups, and why are their activities diminishing? A reason is that, with all the shortcomings of our democratic procedures, our political system provides two ways in which violence is diffused prophylactically before it emerges. The first is the vast network of formal and informal channels through which grievances can be voiced and, at least, given the impression of being considered. The terrorist usually "shoots in the direction from which there is no hope"; in our system, there always seems to be an alternative action promising hope for peaceful settlement of grievances. The second way involves the abundance of opportunities to exercise a relatively high degree of violence without repercussions from society, such as restraint or punishment. Catharsis is provided by sublimation, transference, and diffusion of violent aggression in such socially acceptable modes as sports, televised dramatic violence, and the news media.

The question remains: How to combat terrorism? One may follow the Henri Laborit, French scientist, who maintains that to deal with human violence in general, "a start must be made. . . [to see] that society's rewards no longer go to its least compassionate members. there is no other way . . . to avoid . . . violence, exploitation, warfare, and genocide.

10

Terrorism and High-Technology Weapons

Terrorism—ideological and political violence utilized by subnational groups who seek to achieve imaginary or realistic tactical and strategic objectives—is relevant to the concept of high-technology weapons. The seriousness of this relationship was described succinctly by Justice Arthur J. Goldberg: "Modern terrorism, with sophisticated technological means at its disposal and the future possibility of access to biological and nuclear weapons, presents a clear and present danger to the very existence of civilization itself." Such an awesome eventuality forces us to think about the "unthinkable" with grave concern. This chapter is designed to examine these novel aspects of contemporary ideological and political violence and to focus on the potential threat of nuclear terrorism.

Dangers of Unconventional Terrorism

Pragmatic and symbolic acts—arson, bombing, hostage taking, kidnapping and murder—undertaken by extremist groups for the purpose of pressuring governments and peoples to concede to the demands of the perpetrators already have victimized, killed and maimed thousands of innocent civilians. These casualties include government officials, politicians, judges, diplomats, military personnel, police officers, business executives, labour leaders, university professors, college students, school children, travellers, pilgrims and Olympic athletes. Considerable damage has been inflicted as well on nonhuman targets. Terrorists have attacked government offices and police stations; pubs, restaurants and hotels; banks, supermarkets and department stores; oil pipelines, storage tanks and refineries; railroad stations, air terminals and jetliners; broadcasting stations, computer and data centres and electrical power facilities.

The dictum, "No mass casualties and widespread disruptions of vital systems of industrialized nations have yet resulted from a single terrorist attack" has become obsolete. Terrorist groups usually have used guns and bombs and, only rarely, more sophisticated weapons such as man-portable antitank rockets and ground-to-air missiles when they became available. Having achieved considerable tactical success, terrorists have found it politically and morally expedient to restrain the level of violence. Had it been otherwise, they could have used conventional weapons to cause major disasters in our extremely vulnerable society by attacking, for example, hazardous-chemical plants.

There are; however, no guarantees that the self-imposed constraints of terrorist groups will persist indefinitely and that future incidents will not be much more costly in terms of human lives and property. Three considerations suggest such a probable draconian development. First, assuming that conventional terrorism would be brought under substantial control in the foreseeable future through national and international legislation, as well as through increased security and enforcement measures, this in fact may hasten the advent of mass destruction terrorism. After all, terrorist groups tend, whenever possible, to attack "soft" targets, those without security or any appearance thereof. This world wide trend has been noted clearly over the 1970-78 time span and accounts for an evolution in terrorist targeting from primacy accorded attacks on police and military facilities (1970-72), to a shift toward assaulting diplomatic and related personnel (1973-75), to an emphasis on business targets (1976-78). In each stage, the primary target group selected for assault was less secure and thus easier to attack, than the previous one. Today, however, many business firms are following the lead of police and diplomatic establishments by upgrading their security. As a result, other vulnerable targets created by technological advances of contemporary society are likely to become more attractive to terrorists.

A second consideration for the probable shift from conventional to mass destruction violence is the propaganda and psychological warfare value of such operations to terrorist groups. Since the strategy of terrorism does not prescribe instant victories over adversaries, an extension of the duration and impact of violence is indispensable. As a keen observer stated, "The media are the terrorist's best friend. The terrorist's act by itself is nothing; publicity is all." Should effective governmental and intergovernmental responses deny terrorists their sought-after publicity, they are likely to change tactics, increase their audacity and escalate their symbolically oriented acts through high-technology weapons.

A third consideration that might encourage nonconventional terrorism is the fact that since ideological and political violence is usually a means to an end, it progresses in proportion to the aims envisioned. If the goals are higher, then the level of terrorism necessarily must be higher. The only constraints to such violence are the limits of available weaponry. Thus, it is conceivable that a highly motivated and desperate terrorist group with technological and financial assets will attempt to improve its bargaining leverage by resorting to mass destruction violence. Such a determined group would be willing to take numerous risks in acquiring and using such weapons. Because the confrontation is seen in many groups as an all-or-nothing struggle, in case of failure the terrorists are prepared to bring the government to submission and actually use these weapons, in the process bringing devastation and destruction to many lives including their own. For these terrorists, the fear of deterrence or retaliation does not exist as it does in the case of states.

It is clear that the prospects of success for such a group would be enhanced if it had previously demonstrated high technological capabilities and a strong willingness to incur high risks involved in similar ventures. Even if there were some skepticism about the credibility of the threat. The danger here is that if one subnational body succeeds in achieving its goals, then the temptation for other terrorist groups to use, or threaten to use, similar weapons may become irresistible.

Chemical and Biological Terrorism

In view of these considerations, experts do not exclude the possibility that the arsenal of tomorrow's terrorists might include chemical, biological and nuclear instruments of massive death and destruction potential. These weapons are capable of producing several thousand to several million casualties in a single incident and of causing governmental disruption of major proportions and widespread public panic. Cases of Anthrax disease are being reported in USA and other countries. A panic-like situation has arisen there.

There are inherent differences, to be sure, among weapons of high technology with regard to their characteristics and modes of action. The resort to chemical and biological weapons is more achievable than the use of nuclear explosives; more specifically, no insurmountable technological impediments arise in the utilization of chemical agents (e.g., fluoroacetates, organophosphorus compounds and botulinum toxin). They are relatively easy to obtain, their delivery systems are manageable and their dispersal techniques are efficient. For example, it has recently been reported that "terrorists wanting to make deadly nerve gases can still find the formulas at the British Library despite attempts by the Government to remove them from public access."

Once in possession of such information, a terrorist with some technical know-how could synthesize toxic chemical agents from raw materials or intermediates. In fact, many chemical toxins are commercially available; they could be either bought or stolen. Also, covert and overt options for dispersing chemical agents are virtually limitless: the poisoning of water systems, contamination of food supplies, generation of gases in enclosed spaces with volatile agents, generation of aerosols in enclosed spaces with nonvolatile agents, and dispersal with explosives.

A number of chemical terrorism incidents already have occurred. In 1975, German authorities received the threat that mustard gas, stolen from an ammunition bunker in the country, would be used against the population of Stuttgart unless all political prisoners were granted immunity. Only some of the stolen canisters were later found. In the following year, U.S. postal authorities intercepted a package, presumably mailed by an Arab terrorist group, containing a small charge designed to explode a vial of nerve gas when the package was opened. And more recently, Israeli citrus fruit was contaminated with liquid mercury.

As in the case of chemical violence, biological terrorism—the use of living organisms to cause disease or death in man, animals or plants—is technologically possible. Warfare agents such as brucellosis (undulant fever, coccidioidomycosis (San Joaquin Valley or desert fever) and psittacosis (parrot fever) are easy to acquire, cultivate and disseminate. The poison ricin, for example, is developed from castor beans; only about half a milligram is fatal.

Evidence indicates that terrorists seriously have considered resorting to biological terrorism. In 1970 members of the Weather Underground were planning to steal germs from the bacteriological warfare centre at Fort Detrick, Maryland, for the purpose of contaminating a city water supply; organizers of Rise, a group of young people dedicated to creating a new master race, were arrested in 1972 in a abortive plot to poison Chicago's water system with typhoid bacteria; and in 1975 technical military manuals on germ warfare were found in a San Francisco hideout of the Symbionesse Liberation Army.

Nuclear Terrorism

Notwithstanding the assumption that in the short-term future chemical and biological terrorism is more feasible technologically, nuclear terrorism – the explosion of a nuclear bomb, the use of fissionable material as a radioactive poison and the seizure and sabotage of nuclear facilities – has received far greater public attention. As one observer remarked, "It cannot be assumed that these possibilities have been ignored by existing or potential terrorists or that they will not be considered in the future."

Awareness of this danger is growing. Warnings were issued in the United States and abroad that thefts from nuclear plants might provide terrorists with material to make a crude bomb. Concern also was expressed that the attacks on nuclear power plants discussed in European underground publications may encourage domestic groups to escalate their violence. And more recently, Joseph M. Hendrie, chairman of the Nuclear Regulatory Commission, reported that his "agency has concluded [that] the possibility of terrorist interest in nuclear capability cannot be discounted.

Scholars have provided numerous scenarios of nuclear terrorism over the years. Examples of some of the more obvious possibilities that are technically feasible and politically plausible include the threat or use of a nuclear option by: a group of psychopaths and sociopaths with suicidal tendencies, who use nihilistic violence for its own sake; political or environmental extremists seeking to carry out acts of symbolic violence against nuclear facilities; a revolutionary group acting against its own government or against a foreign country in order to increase pressure on the home government to meet the revolutionaries' demands; a national liberation movement working against the imperialist government in the mother country; or a terrorist group engaged in a proxy war initiated by an outside state or even a nuclear power.

Such developments are indeed serious because they either could result in a broad-scale nuclear war or increase the risk of such a war. This likelihood increases in situations where nuclear terrorism can be used as a form of war by proxy or as a tactical weapon by desperate terrorist groups. It is conceivable, for example, that if Israel were a target of a "surrogate" nuclear attack by the Palestine Liberation Organization (PLO), the United States and the Soviet Union might reach a point of confrontation that greatly increases the dangers of a nuclear war between them.

A major factor encouraging this frightening reality is the profound negative effects of nuclear proliferation, both vertically and horizontally. At present, tens of thousands of nuclear weapons, including tactical ones, are in military stockpiles. Although the current "nuclear club" is limited in membership, it is expected that some forty to fifty nations will have access to peaceful nuclear material and technology by the end of the century. Therefore, it will not be difficult for nations desiring to manufacture their own nuclear weapons to do so. A small processing plant, sufficient to produce enough fissionable weapons-grade plutonium 239 for three or four bombs per year, can be built at the cost of several million dollars. India's manufacture of a nuclear device with technology supplied by Canada and the recent deals between West Germany and Brazil, France and Pakistan and Libya and the Soviet Union involving pilot reprocessing plants certainly chart a new trend.

Other nations on the threshold of nuclear power are Argentina, Egypt, Israel, Iran, South Korea, Taiwan and South Africa. Some nations, such as Indonesia and Turkey, have the motivation to go nuclear but not the capability yet to join the club. There are over a dozen states, for example Austria and Japan, that have the capability but no incentive at the present. We now can project that, by 1990, developing countries alone will be capable of making 3,000 nuclear bombs per year; and at the beginning of the twenty-first century, the world could make more than 100,000 nuclear explosives each year.

This enormous expansion in the nuclear arsenal is indeed alarming, not only because of the total number of weapons stockpiled, but also because most of them will be without the electronic safety locks and coded permissive action links (PALs) protecting weapons of the more advanced nuclear powers. While stealing or seizing a tactical nuclear weapon from a less sophisticated nuclear nation might be more tempting to a terrorist group, an attempt to acquire weapons from the superpowers should not be ruled out. For instance, weaknesses and shortcomings in the security system of some U.S. Armed Forces' storage depots highlight questions of command, inventory control and communications. Furthermore, the transit of nuclear warheads between missile sites improves the chances for success of a terrorist group. Even if the difficulties of detonation of a stolen bomb prove to be insurmountable, the terrorist group still will be able to use the weapon as a credible threat.

The risk of theft or seizure of tactical and strategic weapons at home and abroad has been expressed by many observers. One test scenario describes the seizure of a launch control center at a Minuteman missile site by terrorists, thereby providing them with the capability to launch a nuclear attack. In this particular case, "there is little reason to have confidence that Minuteman safeguards are inviolable."

Even if shortcomings in safeguards and physical security measures of the United States and other advanced nuclear countries were corrected, the fact remains that lesser technological states will not always introduce similar improvements and therefore they still will be vulnerable to seizure or theft of nuclear weapons. In such circumstances, the security of the more sophisticated nuclear states well be in jeopardy. Clearly protection and safety can be improved on all levels, but the risks can only be reduced and not completely eliminated.

As a consequence of the use of the oil embargo and the political unreliability of some oil-producing countries, moreover, industrial nations have been motivated to develop alternative sources of energy. Nuclear power has figured largely in these efforts. Currently, more then 300 nuclear power plants are either operating, under construction, or planned in 26 countries; the vast majority are in the United States. Thus, as the world moves deeper into the plutonium economy, the potential dangers of diversion, theft, or seizure of fissionable nuclear material produced by private industry will become greater.

This vulnerability in the United States and elsewhere already has generated various recommendations on international and national levels to improve the physical protection of nuclear material in civilian hands. Cases in point are the reports, suggestions, guidelines and regulations provided by the International Atomic Energy Agency (IAEA), the Non-Proliferation Treaty Review Conference and the U.S. Atomic Energy Commission. Despite these and other efforts, current international safeguards are totally inadequate. Some analysts have concluded that there "is no systematic exchange among states of technical, administrative, or intelligence information regarding physical protection of nuclear facilities and materials or of information concerning terrorist threat potentials. Similarly, there appears to be no contingency plan for, nor international coordinative mechanism to deal with, a theft of nuclear materials from one state to another."

This vulnerability is expected to turn in the opening up of opportunities for a black market of plutonium, thereby increasing the chances of success in obtaining the needed fissionable material. Only some eleven to twenty pounds of such material are necessary to construct a crude explosive device with a probable yield in the range between several hundreds and several thousands of high explosives. If this device were detonated in a crowded metropolitan area, as many as 10,000 people might be killed directly, while tens of thousands of others might suffer from severe fallout exposure.

With fissionable material available, to be sure, a determined terrorist group wishing to manufacture its own homemade weapon can do so without insurmountable difficulty. As early as the 1960s, various reports indicated that persons using only classified information as well as publicly available literature could design a crude device to function in the nuclear mode. For example, in 1975 an undergraduate at the Massachusetts Institute of Technology designed a workable bomb of low yield. Similarly, in 1976 a Princeton University student put together a design for an explosive with half the power of the Hiroshima yield; the bomb could be built for $2,000. And more recently, at Harvard University an economics major with only one year of physics designed a series of nuclear bombs in five months.

If bright undergraduates have the technological know-how to design nuclear bombs, then it is obvious that any proficient terrorist group who can obtain the fissionable material and do what these students have done will have a reasonable chance of building, quite skillfully and safely, a homemade bomb for $10,000 to $30,000. It is even possible that some of the tens of thousands of scientists, engineers and other trained personnel in the nuclear field might be motivated by political convictions or economic and personal considerations and therefore participate in a nuclear operation. In addition, experts themselves might be kidnapped and forced to contribute their expertise in exchange for their lives or the lives of their families.

Another aspect of nuclear terrorism is the problem of radiological weapons dispersal. A plausible alternative to the explosion or threat of explosion of a nuclear device is the utilization of plutonium or any other radioactive nuclides for the dispersal of radioactivity in any given area, or for the contamination of natural resources. A dispersal threat would be more credible if only because it requires less material and a lower level of technological expertise. Thus, a determined terrorist group could place only 3½ ounces of plutonium (Sb_4 venom or potassium cyanide) in a dispersal device such as an aerosol canister. This could be an effective radiological weapon if introduced into the air conditioning system of a large government office building. The result would be devastating. Several thousand people would die over a period of time depending on the level of dosage absorbed. Additionally, significant psychological effects could create immediate panic and spontaneous mass exodus, resulting in intolerable political, economic and social implications.

Another threat of radioactivity release could occur as a consequence of the sabotage of nuclear power stations. Since an expansion in the number of these stations is expected, the likelihood of such incidents increases. To succeed in such an operation, the terrorists must disable the cooling system to the reactor core of the power station, where radioactive material is contained, thus causing it to melt and release the poisonous substance. Although such a task is more difficult, experts agree that it is not impossible. Once the reactor core melts down, the released material would cause thousands of casualties and serious environmental contamination with both short- and long-term effects. As one observer of nuclear developments has predicted: "Because of its toxic and fissible properties, plutonium offers a unique and powerful weapon to those who are sufficiently determined to impose their will. In these circumstances we do not believe it is a question of whether someone will deliberately acquire it for purposes of terrorism and blackmail, but only of when and how often."

This prediction is not baseless if we examine the historical record. There have already been several hundreds of nuclear-related incidents with serious implications for future trends. Some unclassified examples in the United States, selected at random, include the theft in 1973 of "extremely harmful" capsules of iodine 131 from a hospital in Arcadia, California; the loss in 1969 of a container of highly enriched uranium hexafluoride (UF-6) which was being shipped from Ohio to Missouri; the 1972 threatened crash of a hijacked airliner into the Oak Ridge National Laboratory in Tennessee; the arson at the Indian Point Unit 1977 into the Vermont Yankee Nuclear Power Corp.; the 1976 bomb threat at the B&W naval nuclear fuel facility at Lynchburg, Virginia; and the bomb detonation next to the visitors' center at the Trojan nuclear power plant in Prescott, Oregon, in 1977. Thus far, thousands of pounds of low-enriched uranium and plutonium have disappeared during the past several years. According to a recent report, more than fifty tons of fissionable material was unaccounted for in some thirty-four facilities operated by the Energy Research and Development Administration.

Similar incidents took place overseas: the theft of fuel rods from atomic power stations in England in 1966; the apparent uranium smuggling operation uncovered in India in 1974; and the apparent intrusion attempts, surveillance operations and disturbances at perimeter fences and areas outside nuclear weapons storage sites in Europe. Two cases are worth mentioning. A lone terrorist, calling himself a "justice guerrilla" protesting against prison conditions in

Austria, dispersed radioactive material in two trains in 1974; several people became ill in these incidents, and the perpetrator escaped. During the same year, right-wing Italian terrorists planned to poison the country's water supply with radioactive uranium stolen from a nuclear center; the scheme also involved a plan to assassinate top government officials and the Communist party leader. The alleged purpose of the plot was to create public panic, compel the army to intervene and open the way for a rightist government takeover. The plot was uncovered with the arrest of several members of the group.

Finally, since 1970 there have been a dozen terrorist attacks against nuclear facilities. According to available data, these incidents represent 6.8 per cent of the total 192 terrorist attacks against utilities around the world. For instance, in 1973 members of the Revolutionary Army of the People (Ejército Revolucionario del Pueblo – ERP) seized the nearly completed Atucha nuclear station in Argentina; the attackers escaped after painting a political slogan on the building, stealing weapons and wounding several guards. In 1975 several bombs exploded at the site of a French nuclear power station under construction in Fessenheim, south of Strasbourg; there was some damage, but no significant delay in the completion of the reactor. The "Meinhof-Puig Antioch" group claimed credit for this incident. During the same year two explosions caused minor damage to a nuclear power plant in Brittany; a local separatist group has been suspected of this act of sabotage. Other attacks occurred in 1976 when a group known as Commando d'Opposition par Explosifs a I'Auto-destruction de l'Univers (COPEAU) – or Commando of Opposition by Explosives to the Self-Destruction of the Universe – bombed the Paris offices of a manufacturer of nuclear fuel elements and a uranium mine in southwestern France, causing extensive damage at both locations.

Two incidents are noteworthy more recently. In March 1978, the Basque separatist terrorist organization (ETA) bombed the partially Europe; the bombing caused $8.1 million in damage to the plant killed two workers and injured fourteen. Several months earlier, members of the same group had opened fire at the site but were beaten back by police. And in a related nuclear facility issue, the German Revolutionary Cells have claimed responsibility for a May 1978 explosives attack on a private security firm contracting at a nuclear works site at Kalkar, West Germany and for an incendiary attack on a vehicle belonging to the police chief who handled violent demonstrations at that location.

Limited as these incidents are, they should not be constructed to mean that the world in the years ahead will face isolated cases of nuclear terrorism. It is likely that changing political, economic and social patterns in the domestic and international situations over the next two decades might give rise to pressures and tensions that could motivate terrorists to engage in nuclear terrorism.

Summary

The intrinsically complicated threats arising from any sort of chemical, biological and nuclear terrorism may become an ominous future reality. If modern society is to provide a reasonable degree of protection against super-terrorism, developments in this area of public concern must be monitored continuously and patiently by all involved. Emergency preparedness counter measures necessarily must include contingency planning and sound crisis management policies at various governmental, intergovernmental and non-governmental levels.

Faced with potential dangers of unconventional terrorism, democratic states must ask themselves what price they are prepared to pay, in terms both of expenditures and of diminution of their citizens' convenience and civil liberties.

1) Exceptional measures of law enforcement should be kept to the lowest necessary level.

2) All such measures should be specifically expressed as temporary deviations from the norm. They should be subject to review, renewal and revision.

3) They should be tightly framed so as to ensure that the civil liberties of the people as a whole are affected as little as possible. The use of any special powers should be linked to a discernible and defined threat; such powers should not be available for the suppression of dissident opinion at large.

11

Harbour of International Terrorism: Imperialist Military Bases in the Indian Ocean

The successes of the national liberation struggles in Vietnam, Bangladesh, Middle East and recently in the Portuguese colonies and others have highly contributed to the historical process of disintegrating world imperialism and chiefly the U.S. imperialism. Imperialist military alliances like SEATO in Asia collapsed after the independence of Bangladesh. The entire region of South Asia after the Simla, Delhi and Lahore Agreements is demanding peaceful development free from all outside interference and imperialist military bases. On the other side of the Indian Ocean the most hated Pretoria regime of South Africa has been severely condemned by the entire international community in the United Nations so much so that the British Labour Government had to apologize for its joint naval exercises under the Simonstown Agreement. The unholy alliance in the Southern Africa, so far a stumbling block to liberation struggles, has been reduced from three to two. Bisbon is out of the Pretoria-Salisbury Axis thanks to democratic upsurge in Portugal. Events in the Portugal and in Greece have also shaken the powerful North Atlantic Treaty Organization (NATO).

United Opposition of Afro-Asian Nations Against Military Bases in the Indian Ocean

It is in this background that we shall deal with the burning question of imperialist military bases in the Indian Ocean which are a menace to peace, independence, sovereignty and security of all nations in the region.

France, Britain and United States of America have their military bases in the Indian Ocean islands. And as the pressure for their withdrawal grows stronger, the imperialist powers try to raise new pretexts and seek new avenues for strengthening their bases. The collective voice of non-aligned countries in both the continents of Africa and Asia has grown objecting to the continued presence and further enlarging of military bases in this region. The Organization of African Unity and the Non-Aligned group of nations have reacted to this danger to their security in various conferences.

Among the many African countries affected by the presence of imperialist military bases are Somalia, Tanzania and Madagascar which have expressed their official opposition and strong condemnation of new bases being enlarged like the Diego Garcia. Commenting on the false pretexts advanced by the imperialists, the organ of the Africa Society, *Cairo* (March 15, 1974), writes:

'It is truly surprising to find the big western nations talking of the security of the Indian Ocean at present, whereas they have long held numerous military bases in this area and in the countries overlooking the Ocean, such as the nuclear submarine base in Diego Garcia, which in American though the island is British-owned, the British base in the Maldive Island, the remains of British presence in Mauritius and the French base in Djibouti. Despite all the attempts made by the liberation forces concerning this presence, which is regarded as a blatant phenomenon of imperialism and dependence, calls are being issued at present to reinforce this presence.

'This direct military presence is associated with numerous aspects of provocative measures adopted by Western powers vis-a-vis the non-aligned nations, foremost among which are the military arsenals set up with the racist regimes opposed to African liberation, such as South Africa and Israel, and lately Rhodesia.'

'This is, obviously, a representative reflection of the African opinion. Similarly the independent nations of Asia, especially from the non-aligned group of nations like India, Sri Lanka and Bangladesh have been outspoken in their criticisms of the foreign military bases in the Indian Ocean area. The UN had declared the Indian Ocean as a Zone of Peace by its General Assembly Resolution 2832 (XXVI) dated December 16, 1971 and the present XXIX UN General Assembly Session meeting since September 1974 has on its agenda *'Implementation of the declaration of the Indian Ocean as a Zone of Peace.*

U.S. Objective—Interference in Internal Affairs of Sovereign Nations

At about the same time when the Government of Madagascar addressed a letter to the then UN Secretary-General Kurt Waldheim denouncing the expansion of Diego Garcia military base by U.S.A. as it seriously endangered peace and security in the Indian Ocean, two former Pentagon officials were telling the U.S. Congress that the real reason for the U.S. is to create a 'multi-purpose' base capable of launching air, ground and submarine operations should the need ever arise. They also said that the facilities contemplated would probably include not only an air strip to handle Air forces' giant B-52 bombers, but a naval tender equipped to provide off-shore maintenance to nuclear-powered submarines carrying nuclear missiles.

The testimony also revealed that the Pentagon's Joint Chiefs of Staff, in listing some two dozen contingency needs for Diego Garcia in their original request in 1967, cited such possible U.S. military needs as sending assistance to the Indo-China border, the Indo-Pakistan border, the Burmese-Chinese border and to Indonesia.

The U.S. Navy's top brass Admiral Elmo Zumwalt told a Congressional Committee on March 21, 1974 that the main reason for converting the British atoll to Diego Garcia into a U.S. Indian Ocean military base is to 'provide the ability to influence events in that area. The capability to deploy our military power on the region is an essential element of such influence'.

In this context if one recalls the entry of U.S. Carrier *Enterprise* into the Bay of Bengal during the liberation struggle of Bangladesh in 1971, it will be clear what kind of 'influence' the U.S. administration wants and aims at in this region. The recent revelations in the U.S. press and subsequent admission by President Ford himself about the role of CIA in influencing the events in Chile leading to the massacre of the legally elected president Salvador Allende are enough examples for the people of the developing countries to learn proper lessons.

South Africa in Neocolonialist Gun Boat Diplomacy

It is not a question of the security of one or two nations only. The NATO bases in the Atlantic are linked with the Indian Ocean area because of the world-wide network of U.S. military bases. Right from the western coast of Australia up to the British base of Simonstown in South Africa there are a number of intermediary links on the Cocas Islands, the Chagos Archipelago, the Maldive and Seychelles Islands, Dahran, Bahrein, Ethiopia and other territories.

In the imperialist scheme of neocolonolialist gun boat diplomacy, South Africa has been assigned an important role. The fundamental and irreconcilable antagonism of imperialism to the liberation cause of the Afro-Asian countries that is inevitably aroused by the working out of such a policy was visibly demonstrated during the UN debate on the whole question of relationship with the apartheid regime of South Africa. The meeting underlined the fact that those permanent members of the Security

Council, British, France, and U.S.A., who vetoed the resolution for the expulsion of South Africa from U.N. are the one who have military bases in the Indian Ocean area. It is they who strengthen the South African regime and help it overcome its total isolation in the world in order to use it against the liberation forces. It is being drafted for the police functions of imperialism in the Indian Ocean and South Atlantic. South Africa has been serving as a base against the independent African countries. It is worth remembering that many African and Asian countries have been struggling to overcome the imperialist economic domination. They have taken measures to introduce fundamental socio-economic transformations, including complete or partial nationalization of foreign capital. Here again the neocolonialist way of 'influencing' is kept in mind while setting up military bases surrounding the independent young nations. NATO influence is not confined to Atlantic but extended to Pacific and Indian Ocean as well through the world-wide chain of these military bases.

Threat to Arab Lands: Support to Israel

According to the hearings before the Committee on Foreign Affairs of U.S. House of Representatives on March, 12, 1974 the U.S. Government was using former British naval base at Bahrein as a base for the American Middle East forces. The American contingent at the base was increased in 1972 from about 200 to 260. While Israel has been the vehicle and outpost for the aggression against the Arab peoples and their liberation struggles one can easily see the hand of U.S. imperialism in Middle East crisis by the magnitude of war material being supplied to Israeli aggressors. The activities of the notorious U.S. Sixth Fleet off the coasts of the Arab States in the Middle East crisis is quite well known just as the appearance of the U.S. Seventh Fleet was condemned during the final stages of the Bangladesh liberation struggle. In addition to the American Middle East Force, the U.S. Naval forces in the Indian Ocean are part of the Seventh

(Pacific) Fleet which operate from the Subic Bay base in the Philippines. The flagship stationed at Bahrein and destroyer escorts are on the rotational assignments from other naval units of the Atlantic Fleet.

According to the *Washington Post* the U.S. Communication Station at North West Cape which was commissioned in 1967 pursuant to an agreement signed between the United States and Australia in 1963, is capable of very low-frequency communication with submerged system which includes stations at Honolulu, Guam, the Philippines, Diego Garcia and Asmara (1st January 1974).

Non-Aligned Countries Oppose Ocean Base: Stand of AAPSO

On August 1, 1974 the then Foreign Minister of India Sardar Swaran Singh spoke in the Indian Parliament on the question of Indian Ocean and the base at Diego Garcia. He informed Parliament of the united opposition from littoral states to the military bases in the Indian Ocean and referred to the Lusaka and Algiers conferences of the non-aligned countries. It means that not only the littoral states but there are the non-aligned group of countries collectively, who are voicing protest against militarization of the Indian Ocean by imperialist powers. Fortunately, the labour governments of Australia and New Zealand are also dissentiating from the policies of imperialist powers.

Mr. Yousef El Sebai said: 'The Afro-Asian People's Solidarity Organization joins the Governments and peoples of Tanzania, India, Iraq, Sri Lanka, Bangladesh, Madagascar and other Afro-Asian countries along with peace-loving forces all over the world condemning the decision of the United States of America and United Kingdom in extending military bases around Diego Garcia in the Indian Ocean. It poses a serious threat not only to littoral states but to world peace as well. It creates obstacle for the movement towards lessening international tension.

World public opinion must be mobilized for the liquidation of these imperialist military bases from the continent of Asia and Africa to hasten the victory of liberation struggles in this part of the world.

'The AAPSO has been consistently opposing the chain of imperialist bases which are set up to maintain colonial and racialist regimes as well as fro neocolonialist interference in the internal affairs of the Afro-Asian countries. With the glorious victories of the Vietnamese people, Arab peoples and other liberation movements against fascist regimes in Lisbon, Pretoria and Salisbury – imperialism seeks to devise different ways for interference and exploitation. It is the unity of all anti-imperialist forces in Asia and Africa together with world wide progressive forces which will defeat the neocolonialist nefarious game ..."

Diego Garcia: The Horror

Despite world-wide protests and concern expressed by African and Asian governments and public organizations, the U.S. Senate Armed Services Committee approved a three-billion-dollar budget for military construction in Diego Garcia on August 23, 1974. The widening of the airstrip at Diego Garcia from 8,000 to 12,000 feet is aimed at enabling the giant air tankers to land there for refuelling B-52 bombers. In order to operate Poseidon nuclear-missile carrying submarines in this region, Diego Garcia is considered a vital link in the imperialist network of military bases. What is called U.S. 'National interest' in building this base is in substance a threat to progressive governments in this region and to keep ready the long-range targets against the erstwhile Soviet Union.

To those who are apologists of U.S. policies in this part of the world and to those who banked upon the so-called honey-tongued Kissinger diplomacy, the present entry of the U.S. constellation (consisting of three destroyers at least) into the Indian Ocean must be an eye-opener. For the progressive forces who have been warming long ago, there is no surprise.

When some of the misleading reports were circulated either in the UN or outside it about Soviet naval presence in the Indian Ocean, the Governments of Somalia, India and Democratic Republic of Yemen refuted the charge of granting any military base in the Indian Ocean area. The Government of India also announced that at no time did the Soviet Union ask India for a military base.

So far as the developing countries are concerned they know by their own experience as to which power or powers have been exploiting them politically, economically and culturally and consequently who needs military bases in this region or for that matter in any part of the world.

Frantic Search for Safeguarding Neocolonialist Interests

It has been estimated that the direct capital investment alone made by the U.S. monopolies in the littoral states around Indian Ocean amounts to 10,000 million dollars. These monopolies control, for instance, the major part of the rubber and tin and a substantial part of the other natural resources of these countries. Oil produced in the Arab Gulf Area is transported by them across the Indian Ocean. The littoral countries on the Indian Ocean area possess more than a half of the world's proven oil resources and are the main producers of rubber, tea and of tin ore. It is also worth remembering of the entire debate in the Sixth Special Session of the United Nations on Raw Materials and Economic Development, how the United States and other western nations opposed the developing countries on the question of sovereignty over raw materials and natural resources. Ultimately on May 2, 1974 the UN did adopt a Declaration on a New International Economic Order despite the reservations of U.S. delegation. On the other hand since the successful use of oil as a weapon time and again of military intervention to seize oil wells by force of arms.

At a time when FRELIMO is at the head of provisional government of Mozambique, South Africa has been barred and censured in the United Nations, PLO has been invited to participate in the U.N. debate on Middle East, South Asian subcontinent has started a new phase after the Simla Agreement, and there are hopeful trends to shift away from military alliances in the entire South-East Asian region in the aftermath of Paris Peace Agreement on Vietnam and the Vietiane Agreement on the formation of coalition government in Laos—the whole situation has taken a turn in favour of liberation as against imperialism.

Therefore there is a frantic search for safeguarding the neocolonialist interests—their capital investments, supplies of cheap raw material and above all their enormous profits drained through multinational corporations in this entire region. According to the Hong Kong weekly *Far Eastern Economic Review* the U.S. military-strategic and economic policies in the Indian Ocean region are designed to enable the U.S.A. and its partners of the West to gain control of Asian raw material.

Historic Bandung—Beacon Light for Afro-Asian Nations

The Afro-Asian Solidarity Peoples' Organization which derived its inspiration from the historic Bandung Conference would like to remind fellow delegates and observers to this International Conference that we are meeting shortly before the 20th Anniversary of the first Afro-Asian Conference consolidating the process of liberation and unity of anti-imperialist forces. It is but natural here to remember with gratitude the great Indian statesman and the first Prime Minister of India Pandit Jawaharlal Nehru who along with V.K. Krishna Menon made historic contribution at the bandung Conference nearly two decades ago. Today we can very well benefit by the clarion call of Bandung and carry forward the message of consolidation of liberation forces in the interest of collective Asian security, peace, progress and development of all nations.

The main declaration of Bandung Conference of 29 Afro-Asian states pointed to the organic unity between peace and freedom. There can be no durable peace so long as there are any manifestations of imperialism, racialism and neocolonialism. That is why today when we are considering the danger of imperialist military bases in the Indian Ocean we should take up the issue of independence for all the islands as well as other strategic bases still exploited by imperialist powers. Such is the case of Seychelles, Comoro and Re-union Islands. There is a popular upsurge among the people of these islands to get rid of colonial domination

U.S., British, French Presence on Ocean Islands

Speaking at the Sixth Meeting of the UN Ad-Hoc Committee on Indian Ocean the representative of India raised the issue in the following words:

'We must address ourselves to the status of islands in the Indian Ocean area which are still under colonial domination. The General Assembly determined in its various resolutions that the existence of colonialism is incompatible with peace. Since colonial territories are the victims of foreign aggression, a zone of peace cannot be realized without the elimination of such aggression.'

Actually the colonies are outright military bases. Without these colonies in the Indian Ocean, neither of the three imperialist powers – British, French and U.S.A., could instal their fleet and destroyers. This is the real reason why the British Indian Ocean Territory has been created and an Association Touristique de l'Ocean Indien (ATOI) has been set up which is controlled by South African interests. The economies of Reunion And Seychelles have been made to depend more and more on trade with Southern Africa. That is why France which is a trading partner does not want to leave Reunion where it has its Project Omega. These imperialist powers want to retain control both economically and politically. Military bases infringe and violate first and foremost the liberty of the countries where they are located. It involves the countries concerned in the wars over which they have no direct role in triggering and always pose the threat of internal interference. There is the immediate danger of intervention in the neighbouring region.

Military bases serve as a guarantee, even to weak colonial powers, of continued imperialist support like NATO to Portugal, Spain and Turkey. Similarly Britain has been supporting or conniving with Pretoria and Salisbury regimes. The Simonstown Agreement with South Africa was aimed at linking the military chains against the liberation movements.

Indian Ocean: A Zone of Peace

There is no doubt that the present trend in favour of detente and peaceful coexistence will grow and together with it the demand of 'nuclear-weapon free zones' and 'peace zones' will also grow. The Afro-Asian countries who are struggling for complete political and economic liberation from the clutches of imperialism understand the need of a Peace Zone in the Indian Ocean. They also know that such a Peace Zone can only be materialized when the imperialist military bases are eliminated, military alliances and pacts dominated by imperialist powers are dismantled and there is no outside interference in their internal affairs. The non-aligned movement which gained momentum since the Bandung Conference, has had several conferences since then, like Belgrade, Cairo, Lusaka and Algiers. During the Cairo summit of the non-aligned countries in 1964 leaders from Asia and Africa spoke against imperialist designs of military bases in the Indian Ocean area. Consequently, the

Cairo Conference condemned 'the expressed intention of imperialist powers to establish bases in the Indian Ocean, as a calculated attempt to intimidate the emerging countries of Africa and Asia and an unwarranted extension of the policy of neocolonialism and imperialism.

The same anti-imperialist spirit prevailed and further cemented in the Lusaka and Algiers conferences. As the liberation forces advance, they invariably create conditions for peace whether it is the question of opening Suez Canal or extension of peace zones. The struggle for a peace zone in the Indian Ocean is part and parcel of world-wide struggle for peace and development. The battle for economic independence in other forums like UNCTAD, IMF, UNDP or other UN organs taught the developing countries that while western imperialist powers oppose them in there plans for development, the Soviet Union and other socialist countries support them. In this context, it is worth mentioning that the first and second seminars on oil in Baghdad have helped in rousing the consciousness of people in the developing countries. The progressive movements of the people in the capitalist countries also support the aspirations of the developing nations. Thus, the process which is developing contains in it the seeds of peace zones and the countries of the Indian Ocean region would certainly win peace in this part of the world through the unity of all progressive forces. (*Courtesy:* Aziz Sherif)

12

Terrorism in Historicity: Fascism

More than half a century ago, Sergio Panunzio, who was to serve fro the major part of his life as one of the principal ideologues of Fascism,[1] put together a rationale for political violence.[2] Given the contemporary preoccupation with political violence, that rationale seems to have particular immediate relevance. Our political universe is peopled by groups and fragments of groups committed to political violence as a revolutionary strategy and the number of commissions and conferences devoted to the current problem of contemporary violence and terrorism in legion. To date, all those conferences and commissions have had little success in formulating a definition of violence and terrorism that might serve as the basis for either academic review, theory generation, or effective intervention and legislation.[3]

The first Fascists felt compelled by moral and pragmatic considerations to articulate a rationale for political violence as ancillary to their revolutionary enterprise. By the time Panunzio published his "defense of violence" in 1921, Fascism had fanned out from Ferrara to envelop the whole of Northern Italy in that political violence that marked the penultimate knowledge, only Fascism, of all the revolutionary movements prepared to employ violence in the pursuit of power, provided an argued distinction between "violence" and "terror" that might be of some contemporary cognitive significance.

Neither Karl Marx nor Friedrich Engels were particularly scrupulous about their use of the term "terror". On one occasion Marx insisted that there was only "one way" to shorten the "agonies of the old society and the birth pangs of the new—revolutionary terrorism."[4] Elsewhere he insisted that "force is the midwife of every old society pregnant with a new one,"[5] as though both terror and force might well be the same thing. Engels' discussion of force in his *Anti-Duehring* takes us not a *whit* further in attempting to distinguish violence from terror.[6] In 1982, Marx spoke of force as necessary for revolutionary change, while a commentator on his delivery speaks of Marx's advocacy as an appeal to violence, again as though both terms referred to the same acts.[7]

In a variety of places, both Marx and Engels made reference to "terrorism", sometimes using it as a synonym for individual acts of violence. There are instances when Engels came close to making a significant distinction between violence and terror, but those distinctions were not systematically pursued. Lenin, in turn, seemed to characterize terrorism as "single combat", individual acts of violence "unconnected with the mass of the people". After Lenin, in the exacerbated *polemics* of Karl Kautsky and Leon Trotsky, written about the time that Panunzio was completing his *Diritto, forza e violenza,* one finds both authors moving artlessly between violence and terrorism as though both terms refer to the same behaviors and the same phenomenon.

Even the contemporary academic literature available to us is characterized by a wide variety of usages. E.V. Walther speaks of terror as an emotional state caused by specific acts or threats of violence and terrorism as a compound of three elements: the act or threat of violence, the emotional reaction and the social effects. Barrington Moore refers to violence and terror as "negative compulsions" and at times seems to equate violence with terror. In 1934, J.B.S. Hardman spoke of terrorism as activities involving a "systematic use of violence", but somehow sought to distinguish between "mass insurrection" and the "terrorist method". David Rapoport, on the other hand, speaks of terrorists and terrorism as involving individuals and acts bent on injury and unconstrained by "moral limits" and consequently argues that a moral distinction can be made between acts of political violence in general and terrorism *per se*.

Given all this, Panunzio was singularly modern in terms of his analysis. He advanced an account far more sophisticated than any found in Marxist and much of the contemporary academic literature. In the first place, he attempted to formulate an analysis that distinguished between the exercise of force and the employment of violence. Force, for Panunzio, was a generic term that referred to what we now identify with power, the ability to alter individual and collective behaviors in the service of given purpose. Alterations of such behaviors can be the function of either normative, material, or coercive force (or power). *A* can alter *B's* conduct by persuasion, by primary or secondary socialization, by restricting his access to some one or another welfare benefit, or by the threat or reality of coercion.

Normative, material, or coercive force manifests itself via socially sanctioned ("legitimate") instrumentalities: the communications media, the schools, rule-governed codes of conduct, entrance criteria into the professions, the legal system, the armed forces of public security and the institutions of detention and punishment, among others. Positive law holds all of this together and constitutes the sinews of institutionalized force.

Violence, in turn, is the perfect analogue of force except that its activities do not possess established social sanction and its behaviors do not represent positive, but potential, law. The distinction between force and violence, for Panunzio, rests in the fact that force represents the interests of the present social system. Like force, violence seeks to alter individual and collective behaviours thought the employment of normative persuasion, material sanctions and incentives and coercive disincentives. Revolutionary propaganda attempts to influence rational calculation and moral deliberation. Revolutionary trade and political organizations attempt to provide the incentives that prompt men to accord their behaviors to those of the revolutionary collectivity. Coercion is directed against the "counter-revolutionary enemy", against whom the revolution undertakes "internal war".

Panunzio conceived of force and violence as perfect analogues. Established society makes war, use coercion, against criminals, subversives and external enemies. Revolutionaries, similarly, make war against counter-revolutionaries, the agents of governmental despotism and all declared "internal enemies". For Panunzio, both force and violence were sanctioned by moral principles. Force is employed to assure a common unanimity of opinion concerning certain group-sustaining values—the security of life, possessions, national integrity, continuity of government and the provision of necessary welfare. Violence appeals to an alternative set of priorities, an alternative future, a potential reality, more capable of providing the creature and moral satisfactions than the present social system is. In substance the difference between "force" and "violence" (a different first suggested by Georges Sorel) is the difference between alternative social futures. The justification for either must necessarily be the consequence of rational calculation.

Just as external wars are never (or should never be) undertaken without the most rigorous factual and moral calculation, internal wars, coercive power, can only be employed in the service of ends that promise the realization of some ultimate good unattainable by any other means. Wars, the employment of coercive and deadly force and coercive and deadly violence, are undertaken for just such moral ends. Only enough coercive power can be employed that will secure such ends.

In this sense, Panunzio, like the Marxists, in general, makes ultimate appeal to an anticipated future ("history") as providing the moral justification for the use of coercion. Thus, Trotsky sought to justify Boshevik violence by an appeal to "the fact that the proletariat [was] the historically rising class" and that the "bourgeoisie is a falling class". The bourgeoisie was the proper object of violence, since it was "destroying the economic structure of the world and human culture generally."

Unlike Trotsky and like Karl Kautsky, Panunzio rejected the notion that any means are justified by a good end. Panunzio, like Kautsky, insisted that moral ends cannot justify immoral means. Given this caveat, Panunzio, like Kautsky, was prepared to attempt to draw a line between *"licit"* and *"illicit"* individual and collective coercion. Panunzio's arguments were more rigorously developed than those of Kautsky. Panunzio sought to define violence in such a fashion that criminal and morally objectionable acts might be distinguished from those licensed by some moral precept or some effective procedural rules.

Panunzio argued that there could be crimes committed in the course of both external and internal war. Individuals who, in war or revolution, take advantage of unsettled circumstances to employ force and violence for personal advantage threaten both the moral integrity of their enterprise and the viability of the community itself. Both governments at war and revolutionary leadership have been historically prepared to recognize the existence of such criminal behaviors and both (ideally) punish offenders in their own ranks. Rape, looting and murder have always been recognized as punishable offenses by governments, the organized military and the leadership of revolutionary forces. These constitute, for Panunzio, "criminal acts in war".

Panunzio was prepared to recognize another class of criminal acts in war, acts he identified as *"war crimes"* and their perpetrators as *"war criminals"*. Those acts are calculated behaviors, ordered by an established leadership, that wreak havoc, death and injury on *innocents,* noncombatants, women, children, the old, the unarmed and the generally helpless. The aim of war is to bend the enemy to our will. For that purpose deadly force is employed. The enemy takes up arms in his own defense and in the effort to bend us to his will. Against such an enemy, deadly force is appropriate. All modern nations, on the other hand, recognize that an unarmed enemy can no longer be the object of deadly force (just as the police recognize that an unarmed fugitive, no matter how heinous his crime, is no longer the proper object of deadly force). Enemy soldiers are not "innocent". They have made it their sworn intention to use deadly forces against our soldiers similarly sworn. But an unarmed enemy, like an unarmed murderer, is no longer the proper object of deadly force. He may be guilty, but he is helpless. He is a prisoner of war, or a police captive and expects every protection that status accords. By extension of these principles, Panunzio argued that unarmed civilians, the old, infirm, the children, because of their innocence and helplessness, cannot be the proper objects of deadly force.

When such deadly force is directed against such victims, the act, for Panunzio, was an act of terror. [The act of terror, in its most manifest expression, is an act of *severe coercion,* frequently an act of deadly force, directed against an *innocent* victim or victims, in which the victim or victims is instrumental (a means) to the furtherance of some *proximate end* (for example the generation of fear or intense anxiety on the part of others).] Panunzio seems to have felt that only acts that satisfy these conditions can be identified as acts of terror, morally prescribed acts of coercion.

Thus, the employment of means for indiscriminate destruction, such as poison gas, saturation bombing and shelling of population centers of no appreciable military significance, biochemical and mass destruction devices, would qualify by such criteria, as "terroristic" and consititute "war crimes". Panunzio identified such acts with illustrations from this contemporary experience. The long-distance and indiscriminate shelling of Paris by German artillery, the Zeppelin bombing of London and the use of asphyxiant gas on the Western Front, were all condemned by Panunzio as criminal acts of terrorism.

According to his account, Panunzio would not characterize the public and often brutal execution of criminals in time of peace as terroristic even if at least part of the intention was to deter such acts, that is, even if such public executions were employed to instil fear and anxiety among the general population. The criminal, in such an instance, although helpless, was not an innocent. He was (presumably) guilty of a crime. Similarly, the use of deadly force, not terroristic because soldiers are not innocents. The sworn duty of a combatant involves the use of deadly force against us. Moreover, the combatant can his purpose by surrender and then, once helpless, is accorded whatever protection the rules of war provide.

By implication, the use of deadly force against noncombatants in time of war is an act of terror. The victims of such deadly force are innocents. There is no specific piece of voluntary behaviour on their part that would reduce the probability of their death or injury. In such cases, the use of deadly force is indiscriminate – the deaths of some innocents would do as well as the deaths of others – and its victims are used as means to the accomplishment of proximate ends: demonstrative or illustrative effect.

When Panunzio became involved in the violence of the Fascist revolution, as that violence radiated out of Ferrara, he forever attempted to characterize that violence in terms of his analysis. Similarly, when Curzio Malaparte, years later, attempted an analysis of the Fascist revolution, he characterized it as an "internal war", governed by the strategy, tactics and moral scruples of such wars. Whenever Mussolini referred to instances of Fascist and non-Fascist violence, he regularly invoked distinctions made by Panunzio.

At the commencement of hostilities in northern Italy, Fascist apologists insisted that an "internal war" had been declared against their political opponents. Their enemies were armed and committed opponents lodged in Socialist and Communist organizations – the Leagues, the Chambers of Labor, the fighting squads and the political organizations of the Socialists and Communist Parties. Their enemies had *chose* to be members of such associations and consequently were identified as "soldiers" in the enemy camp and the proper objects of revolutionary violence, including (under appropriate circumstances) deadly force.

What resulted was very much like a civil war. From the 1st of January through April 7th, 1921, for example, violence in Italy claimed 102 lives, among them 25 Fascists and 123 Socialists. The violence was neither one-sided nor directed against unarmed opponents. When the Socialists documented Fascist violence, that violence was almost always directed against victims and institutions that the Fascists had identified as "culpable": determine political opponents and the specific political institutions that housed them. The acts of terror identified by the left-wing opponents of Fascism in 1924, were almost all not acts of terror, but (by Panunzio's definition) *criminal acts* undertaken in the course of insurrectionary violence by individual Fascists in the pursuit of selfish ends, personal profit, the discharge of personal grievances and simple acts of vengeance. All were equally culpable by Fascism's own announced standards of conduct.

The point here is not that Fascists satisfied the requirements of the rationale concerning violence that presumably subtended their activities. It is that their violence was possessed of principles they themselves had formulated. Although those principles were probably more honored in the breach than in the observance, the fact that those principles were bruited distinguishes Mussolini's Fascism from the acts of deadly force perpetrated by the terrorists with which we have become increasingly familiar. Thus, when Carlos Marighella spoke of "terrorism [as] an arm the revolutionary can never relinquish", he meant precisely that. In this regard Marighella spoke of kidnapping "personalities who are known artists, sports figures, or are outstanding in some other field, but who have evidenced no political interest", in order to make their suffering "a useful form of propaganda". Thus, he spoke of kidnapping and if necessary "executing", "North American residents", innocent and unarmed, to make some point or another, or to achieve some advantage in the "war of nerves" against the "establishment".

What Marighella clearly advocated was terrorism: the use of severe sanction or deadly force against innocents for the express proximate purpose of bending others to his will. Given this strategy, terrorist bands commit themselves to the indiscriminate bombing of public buildings, the random downing of civilian aircraft in transit, the kidnapping of innocents to serve as hostages or examples. The difference between Mussolini's Fascists and terrorists is that while Fascist may have undertaken such acts, those acts were understood, by their own standards, as prima facie criminal. For terrorists such a distinction does not obtain. Thus, Fanz Fanon could advocate the murder of any "colonialist", presumably man, woman, or child, in order to restore the impaired self-esteem of an oppressed colonial: deadly force exercised against an unarmed innocent for proximate purpose.

The distinction between Fascist acts of violence and a strategy of terror seems reasonably clear. The members of the Socialists Leagues, the Chambers of Labor, or the Socialist and Communist Parties in Northern Italy during the wave of Fascist violence in the biennial 1921-22 could avoid violence by abandoning the Leagues, the Chambers and the infrastructural institutions of Socialism and Communism. Their compliance with Fascist demands could make them reasonably confident that their immediate security was assured. Their "guilt" was function of their voluntary behavior. They had chosen to behave in a prescribed manner. Their rehabilitation would turn on a specific schedule of compliance behaviors. Similarly, their "innocence" would have been the consequence of a voluntary avoidance of prohibited conduct. In effect, Fascists were prepared to operationalize "guilt" and "innocence" by providing a guide to prescribed conduct. Both "guilt" and "innocence" involved some determinate voluntary acts on the part of the individual or individuals.

Thus, the threat of violence might *intimidate* in order to bend a "guilty" individual, or individuals, to our will—when that individual or those individuals are aware of what specific behaviors will reduce the threat of injury or loss. Terrorism, on the other hand, does not intimidate its victims because it offers them no escape from deadly coercion or loss. There is no schedule of behaviors to which the prospective victim might conform. The victim is an "innocent"—he has neither done anything prescribed nor can be undertake compliance behaviors to avoid threat.

In the course of political revolution, one may intimidate those whose behaviors one wishes to modify. Terror, on the other hand, is not employed to alter the conduct of its victims. It is employed to alter the conduct of its victims. It is employed to influence others. Innocents are used as means to proximate ends.

Thus, severe coercion, even deadly force, on this analysis, used against individual landlords, capitalists, or leaders of Socialist or Communist organizations during insurrectionary phases are acts of political intimidation. By some standard, known to all parties, revolutionaries, landlords, capitalists and political opponents, some voluntary behaviors are proscribed and other voluntary behaviors are prescribed. Compliance behavior is the saving response to such intimidation. Individual behaviors are conceived as relevant to the onset and *termination* of real or potential sequence of violence.

The circumstances are entirely different in the case of terror. In such cases, there is no voluntary behavior that makes the individual the proper object of terror. Any individual or individuals, irrespective of anything they may or may not choose not to do, can become the objects of terror. Nor is there any compliance behavior that would reduce the probability of their falling victim of terror. The object of terroristic violence is not a select and proper object. Terroristic violence has as its purpose not coercive sanction directed against culpable parties, but some proximate end. *Instrumental terror* is employed to impair the functioning of some system or institution. *Demonstrative terror* is used to bend entire populations to the purpose of others. *Prophylactic terror* is employed in anticipation of resistance or rebellion. *Incidental terror* involves those criminal acts—assaults, armed robbery, kidnapping and so on—that impact upon innocent victims in the service of the perpetrator's pathology, profit, or advantage.

One of the most salient traits of terrorism is its *indiscriminate* and *arbitrary* character, in the sense that there is no piece of voluntary behavior that would increase or decrease the probability of finding oneself the object of terror. Terrorist acts are like natural catastrophe—they strike anyone, the guilty and the innocent alike. There are few precautions that one might take to avoid becoming the object of terror. Its onset is incalculable and its termination unpredictable for those who are its victims.

A revolutionary movement or an institutionalized regime may use political intimidation on a small or a large scale. In this respect a measure of the safeguards protecting dissidence, and political opposition, might serve as an index of intimidation and aid in characterizing a movement or regime as repressive or nonrepressive. In a repressive regime, individuals or groups of individuals can successfully avoid severe sanction by compliance behavior. For example, political anti-Fascists could avoid violence during the wave of Fascist intimidation during the biennial 1921 and 1922 by abandoning the Leagues, the infrastructural institutions and political associations of Socialism and Communism. Subsequently the institutionalized regime proceeded to intimidate Catholic and liberal interest groups and political associations. The range of intimidation that typified the political system under Fascist rule could identify it as repressive, but not terroristic. The victims of repression reduce their exposure to violence by compliance behaviour. The victims of terror can do nothing to reduce the probability of their involvement in arbitrary and indiscriminate violence. Instrumental, prophylactic and demonstrative terror uses its victims for proximate ends. It does not select its victims, nor can their behavior influence terrorism's course or termination.

The distinction has clear implications. In a regime of repression victims must evidence at least the semblance of probative guilt. Every system, no matter how libertarian, reserves the right to employ some form of repression, the suppression of dispositions or indispositions to behave in proscribed or prescribed political fashion. What distinguishes one from the other are the effective statutory and traditional restraints upon its exercise. Thus, on the 25th of

November 1926, a Special Tribunal for the Defense of the State, whose transparent purpose was the indimation of political opponents, was instituted trials with few of the legal and procedural safeguards afforded defendants in pluralistic environments. But for all that, each victim was conceived of, in some diffuse sense, as guilty of having undertaken some reasonably specific behaviors, known to all, that the regime considered inimical to its interests. From 1926 until 1943, with the collapse of the regime, the Special Tribunal meted out 47 capital sentences, beginning in 1928 with the sentence of death fro Michele Della Maggiora, who was charged and convicted of assassinating two members of the Fascist militia. Not all of the capital sentences were in fact carried out. From 1928 until 1932 seven death sentences were executed.

Of the lesser sentences, of the 5,619 defendants bound over to the Tribunal between 1928 and 1943, 4,596 were found guilty in varying degrees and 998 were exonerated. With the advent of total war, the charges and the sentences became increasingly capricious and onerous. By 1941 a number of persons were charged with "defeatism", that is, with the voicing of sentiments contrary to the war then in progress. The sentences meted out to such persons were evidently instances of *demonstrative intimidation.*

For all that, the Tribunal, which clearly violated the procedural rules of justice prevalent in liberal democracies, was qualitatively different from institutionalized terrorism. In this respect, Hannah Arendt spoke of the "surprisingly small number and the comparatively mild sentences meted out to political offenders" in Fascist Italy as evidence of the absence of terror. However repressive such as system might have been, it did not qualify as a system of terror.

In order to establish the evident distinction one need only review the circumstances involved in Soviet and national Socialist terror system. In the Soviet Union, for example, severe punishment, including "corrective labor," which for all intents and purposes meant death in a labor camp, could be meted out by the administrative organs of the state, in effect, the NKVD. Thousands, hundreds of thousands of persons passed through the Special Boards in the Soviet Union. Before such boards defendants had no right whatsoever to defense and cases were brought in absentia and against entire groups of persons. Those who could be charged included "members of the family of a traitor to the fatherland," and others who were "suspected of espionage." It was not necessary to establish that defendants had done anything specific, only that they were members of a "tainted" family or were suspected of espionage. Thus, the Basic Criminal Code, Article 22 of the Principles of Criminal Jurisdiction of the Soviet Union of 1937, in a clause unique in international jurisprudence, reads: "Punishment in the form of exile can be applied by a sentence of the State Prosecutor against persons recognized as being socially dangerous, without any criminal proceedings being taken against these persons on charges of comming a specific crime or of a specific offense and, also, even in those cases where these persons are acquitted by a court of the accusation of committing a specific crime."

By 1937 about 10 per cent of all those charged by the extrajudicial administrative bodies were receiving death sentences. Andrei Vyshinsky, in charge of the system during the period, maintained that "When it is a question of annihilating the enemy, we can do it just as well without a trial." In Gorki alone it is estimated that from 50 to 70 persons were executed each day without the semblance of a trial and for the most obscure reasons. By 1938, 5 percent of the total population was involved, and arrests and punishments were applied indiscriminately. By 1938 there was a call for systematic attack on the "silent," those who had not taken any actions during the events of the preceding years. Relatives of "traitors," sometimes singularly remote, were often arrested and shot. There was never any suggestion that they had participated in any way in counter-revolutionary or anti-government activities. The characteristic question asked by victims of the Soviet terrorism was "Why?" The arrests and punishments meted out by the administrative organs and special tribunals under Stalin were not undertaken to identify and punish those who had been guilty of any specifiable offense, no matter how innocuous. Often officials of such organs were simply instructed to arrest a given number of counter-revolutionaries, members of the bourgeoisie, or "kulaks." They were often not given the least indication of the criteria by which such arrests should be undertaken, or on what evidence punishment should be accorded.

Soviet terrorism was clearly demonstrative and prophylactic in intention. Its victims were indiscriminately selected from ill-defined classes of Soviet citizens. They were either known to be innocent of any crime (having been found not guilty by a duly constituted Soviet court), or they were never charged with any offense. There was nothing potential victims might do in order to increase their security against arrest. Soviet terrorism in the military involved leaders down to regimental command. Most of the men who became its victims were men known to be loyal and patriotic Soviet citizens.

There was nothing like this in Fascist Italy. Fascism was not a terroristic but a repressive political system. Its victims were the objects of intimidation, not terror. Only with the anti-Semitic campaign of 1938 did Fascist Italy give evidence of a disposition to employ anything like terror as a political instrumentality.

Racial discrimination harbors some of the principles species traits of terrorism. In general, victims of such discrimination, are subject to social sanction without regard for personal culpability. Since racial traits are ascriptive, there is nothing in principal that an individual can actively do to avoid social and political sanction once such traits are used to identify those subject to differential treatment.

Fascist legislation in 1938, identified anyone, born of Jewish parents, a Jewish father, or of mixed parentage who professed the Jewish religion as a member of the Jewish community and hence subject to discriminatory treatment. Particularly painful was the treatment accorded "Jewish Fascists," those Jews who had been loyal Fascists during the regime but who found themselves threatened by anti-Semitic legislation.

Action was undertaken against an entire category of persons, identified only by ascriptive traits—traits for which they could not have been responsible. Such persons were subjected to economic and professional deprivation, and to public and personal humiliations of a variety of sorts. Whether such acts involved "severe coercion" depends on how one chooses to distinguish between "severe," "onerous," or "burdensome." Such racial legislation, of course, is not unknown to democratic systems. Legislation against the Japanese on the west coast in the United States, and legislation against blacks, was indiscriminate, and produced "burdensome" and even "onerous" disabilities for its victims. Clearly unjust, such legislation may or may not qualify as terroristic when compared with the National Socialist treatment of Jews.

In the case of Fascist Italy such legislation was clearly directed against innocents in order to effect proximate purpose (most probably to cement the alliance with National Socialist Germany). The question remains whether such legislation qualified as severe coercion.

As a matter of act, Fascist anti-Semitic legislation did not produce the mass executions that are now identified with National Socialist persecutions. When the Fascist persecutions were at their climax, 7,495 Jews were deported from Italy. Of that number 6,885 perished at the hands of the National Socialists. None was executed by Fascists, and the question of Fascist complicity in the deportations has no itself been resolved.

In substance, Fascist treatment of the Jews was always attended by some restraint (given the example of Soviet and National Socialist practices). Because Fascist legislation allowed for "mitigations," involving voluntary acts on the part of Jews, discrimination actively fell upon about 20 to 25 percent of those potential objects of anti-Semitic legislation. Those Jewish families, for example, who had lost a member or who had a relative who was a volunteer in the World War I, or who had received decorations for bravery during that conflict, or those who had relatives who had fallen in the cause of Fascism, or had taken part either in the Fiume expedition or the March on Rome, or who had been members of the party before 1924, were relieved of many of the disabilities.

Furthermore, many Jews were "aryanized," declared protected against discriminatory legislation because of some collection of personal behaviors. Conformance behavior could, as Paolo Orano early suggested, provide some small measure of security against political oppression. The number so "aryanized" constituted about 75 percent of those requesting such dispensation. Although the numbers were small (148 in 1941, 163 in 1942, for example), there were provisions for the recognition of voluntary behaviors in the determination of "culpability."

The distinction between Soviet and National Socialist terror, and the oppressive system employed in Fascist Italy, hinged on the recognition that voluntary behaviors had some influence on the treatment of victims. While it is transparent that the treatment of an entire class of persons as guilty, with "innocence" established by some determinate set of compliance behaviors, is clearly in violation of our standards of justice, the fact that voluntary behaviors, in however peripheral a fashion, entered into the meting out of sanctions seems to have mitigated the Fascist system, allowing Fascist anti-Semitism to fall somewhere between terrorism and oppression.

It is interesting to note that the entire racist policy of Fascism was the object of considerable reservations on the part of some of the principle ideologues of the movement. Giovanni Gentile, often identified as the "philosopher of Fascism", clearly objected to its provisions. Panunzio himself left little that was specifically addressed to anti-Semitic legislation, although he did speak of "racism" as a political policy with some approval. In act, Fascist policy could be incorporated into Fascist ideology only with considerable conceptual, theoretical and moral tension. This was particularly true with respect to Fascism's treatment of the Jews.

It seems reasonably clear that for all its stupidities, bestialities and injustices, Fascist anti-Semitism only approximated a policy of terror. The system remained by and large repressive and oppressive rather than terroristic. Its principal negative controls were exercised through intimidation and manipulation. This could be said of its entire insurrectionary program before its advent to power, as well as the operation of the system once ensconced.

All of this argues for a distinction between Fascist repression and oppression however unjust and *barbarous* and consciously undertaken policies of terror in which the purpose of the act is to inflict severe coercion on innocents for some proximate target purpose. In general, Fascist repression was designed to effect changes in conduct on the part of specific individuals adjudged guilty by some reasonably specific criteria. Its purpose was to compel conformity on their part and secondarily on the part of the general population. A terrorist act pursues the same secondary goal but uses innocents as its victims. The distinction between victims can be clearly discerned between the torture of an editor of an opposition newspaper and the death of a housewife in the commission of a terrorist bombing. For the terrorist anyone who is a member of society and not a member of his "revolutionary community", is "guilty" of "complicity" with the "establishment", and hence exposed to his violence. Given this characterization, no compliance behaviors can insulate the potential victim from the outrages of the terrorist. Given the latitude, terrorists will often make their own members the objects of terror for some obscure purpose.

Guerrilla attacks on military personnel and military bases can be taken as acts of "internal war" and at best understood as instances of revolutionary violence. But there is every difference between a selected military target, however remote from any "battle line" and the downing of a civilian between assassinating a representative of an "oppressive" regime (an eventuality Umberto of Italy once called a professional risk of the trade) and the shooting of hostages who just happen to be available to the terrorist.

Notes

1. See A.J. Gregor, *Sergio Panunzio, il sindacalism ed il fondamento razionale del fascismo,* (Rome: Volpe, 1978).
2. The principal work by Panunzio devoted to Fascism's conception of political violence is *Diritto, forza e violenza* (Bologna: Cappelli, 1921). Some relevant discussion is found in Panunzio's pre-Fascist work, *La persistenza del diritto* (Pescara: Abruzzese, 1910) and a work published after his adherence to Fascism, *Lo stato di diritto* (Ferrara: Taddei, 1922).
3. See C. Johnson, "Perspectives on Terrorism", in W. Laqueur (editor), *The Terrorism Reader* (Philadelphia: Temple University, 1978), pp. 267-285.
4. K. Marx and F. Engels, "Sieg der Kontrerevolution zu Wien", *Werke* (Berlin: Dietz, 1959), V, 457.
5. K. MARX, *CAPITAL* (MOSCOW: FOREIGN LANGUAGES, 1954), I, 751.
6. F. Engels, *Anti-Duehring: Herr Eugen Duehring's Revolution in Science* (Moscow: Foreign Languages, 1962), pp. 219-254.
7. See M. Evans, *Karl Marx* (Bloomington: Indiana University, 1975), p. 137.

13

Experiments in Combating Terrorism

In recent years, there had been several bombings in London–in restaurants, pubs (as British taverns are known), the car in which Caroline Kennedy was to ride. Londoners were jumpy and uneasy. Many people were refusing to go into central London at all. The restaurant business and theater attendance were suffering. Then, in accordance with its latest threat, the IRA struck. A bomb went off in the subway. Another exploded in the Ideal Homes Exhibit, with devastating effect. Both bombings coincided with the opening of the tourist season in London. The IRA seemed not only able to terrorize Londoners at will, but also to have a serious economic impact by frightening away tourists who provide foreign exchange and create many jobs in Britain's shaky economy.

The British government reacted with a series of extraordinary measures never before attempted on such a scale. In a way, it became the Battle of Britain all over again. During World War II, Nazi Germany had tried to bomb Britain into submission. The British reacted with typical pluck, and their determination to fight on had only increased. Now, with a handful of Irish bombers threatening London, British pluck asserted itself again. This national characteristic of good humored courage in the face of physical danger was at the root of Britain's antiterrorism campaign.

Signs went up in all the subways and buses instructing riders to look for any abandoned parcels or briefcases. If one was seen, riders were *not* to pull the emergency cord, for this would endanger subway riders. They were to report the parcel at the next station, then all passengers were to leave the train calmly. Such was the public cooperation with this that my casual, nonsuspicious glance at the briefcase at my feet led its owner to reassure me that it was all right.

Since the bomb in the Ideal Homes Exhibit had been deposited in a wastebasket, all trash containers, all storage lockers, all places where a bomb could be planted were removed. London got a little dirtier in terms of litter, but it was no longer easy to find a place to plant a bomb.

Since the bomb at the exhibit had been small, weighing only two pounds, and no larger than a pack of cigarettes, it could easily be carried in a pocket and left in a public place. Therefore, extensive search procedures were undertaken. All persons entering public buildings were undertaken. All persons entering public buildings were searched–quite thoroughly. Both men and women were padded down or frisked. Bulgy articles such as cigarettes or cameras had to be shown. All parcels, including purses, were opened and inspected. It took some time. There were often long lines at the British Museum, Tower of London, theatres, and other public places, But the actions were accepted with good humor. Wry jokes were made about the frisking being a "free massage." Both the British and the tourist knew the search was for their own protection.

The number of police and uniformed guards on duty was increased, and all were extremely watchful for unusual behavior. Everyone was bomb conscious. Because of the IRA penchant for placing bombs in parked cars, parking was restricted and surveillance maintained on unknown or suspicious vehicles. The British people were asked to report any suspicious people living in apartments. Scotland Yard was inundated with reports, and all were investigated.

Law-enforcement officials stepped up their intelligence and surveillance activities. All parcels, including luggage and handbags being brought into Britain from Ireland, were X-rayed. Police closely observed or questioned all know IRA members or sympathizers among the large Irish population in England, In a series of raids, police seized several caches of weapons and explosives.

In those ways, the IRA threat to Britain was defused. No other bombings occurred during the spring, summer, and fall. England had one of its most successful tourist seasons in years. The IRA was seriously set back in England, its weapons and explosives seized, its members harried. Most of all, the British endeavor proved that no nation need be at the mercy of terrorists and that terrorism can be curtailed with minimum inconvenience to the public and without diminution of civil liberties. Police-state repression in the name ot antiterrorism is simply not necessary to combat bombers and gunmen.

The terrorists, striking at innocent people, burst with sudden ferocity on an unprepared world in the early 1970's. They seemed to be able to attack at will. But by 1976, some effective defenses had begun to be used.

The commercial-aviation industry, once the most vulnerable to terrorist attacks, perhaps led the way in thwarting them. The airline defense began with the difficult realization that the days of carefree, unrestricted air travel had to end. Extraordinary measures had to be taken to protect passengers and planes. The first effort was the placement of armed "air marshals" on planes to "ride shotgun." This proved unsuccessful. Airline ticket agents and other personnel were then given detailed instructions, including psychological "profiles" of suspicious people to look for. Anyone even making a joke about carrying a bomb on board was picked up by police and charged with malicious mischief. Careful searches of all passengers hand luggage were begun.

All of these measures, in effect by 1972, were insufficient. Terrorist attacks on planes stepped up in frequency and ghastliness. Expensive metal-detection and X-ray equipment was installed. All passengers entering a loading area had to pass through electronic gadgets and turn out all coins, cigarette lighters, pens, and other metal objects in their pockets. This prevented the bringing of guns and bombs aboard the planes. The ability of terrorists to commandeer the plane in flight was diminished–but as we shall see, not ended.

The Lod Airport massacre showed another weakness. The weapons were flown in with the luggage, then used on the passengers in the terminal. To combat this, all luggage began to be X-rayed.

Terrorist attacks on planes and passengers were now made difficult, so a new tactic was employed. Terrorists began to attack the airports themselves, seizing the planes on the ground. The attack at Rome's airport was as frightful an example as any. To combat this threat, government and airport authorities began to apply extraordinary measures aimed at airport security. Armed guards were employed, then increased in number. On occasion even soldiers and tanks were employed. Entire airports were fenced in and patrolled. Electronic detection devices were installed. Checkpoints were set up for all incoming vehicles. Parking, even loading and unloading, was prohibited at the terminal. Storage lockers and other receptacles for bombs were removed. Closed-circuit television and other surveillance and alarm systems were installed in terminals.

Such measures cannot be 100 per cent successful, but by 1976 there was a sharp reduction in the number of skyjackings and terrorist incidents involving aviation. The measures have been inconvenience to travelers. The electronic equipment and security precautions have been extremely expensive. But they do indicate that terrorism can be curbed and prevented.

When they were first sent out, letter bombs were a dreadful menace, largely because most people did not know such devices were possible and were not expecting them. There were initial casualties, because of the surprise, then defensive measures were taken. Post-office employees now X-ray or use metal-detection devices on suspicious-looking letters and parcels. Still, the random nature of recipients–terrorists simply pick out names from a directory–makes this a continuous threat. Citizens can protect themselves with a few sensible precautions. These were published by the London police commissioner in an article entitled "Danger! Postman Coming!" in the *National Review* of February 2, 1973.

1. Examine the postmark or name of sender. Be suspicious if it is not a known correspondent.
2. Look at the handwriting of the sender. Be careful if the writing is of a foreign style not usually encountered.
3. Balance the letter in your hand. The letter bomb may be lopsided.
4. Judge the weight. Is the weight too heavy for the size?
5. Feel for springiness in the top, bottom, or sides of the letter. Be careful, however, not to bend it excessively.
6. Look for protruding wires. This may occur if the bomb was damaged in transit.
7. Plastic explosives sweat. Look for greasy marks on the envelope or package wrappings.
8. Smell it. Be warned if it smells like almonds or marzipan, a pastry made from almond paste.
9. Gently shake it. If there is the sound of loose pieces of metal, let the bomb squad handle it.

Precautions like these have held down casualties from letter bombs and reduced the effectiveness of this terrorist weapon. Progress has also been made in tightening building security. New, sophisticated alarm systems have been installed. Closed-circuit television is now used routinely to enable a single guard to monitor the public portions of a building. A great many more guards are employed. There are regular patrols of the building. Sometimes dogs trained to sniff out explosives are used. Often now, all people entering a building are stopped, searched, asked to state their business, then accompanied by security personnel to the appropriate office.

Company employees are now instructed in action to take if they find a bomb.

1. Report the location and accurate description of the object to the police.
2. Put sandbags or mattresses around the suspected bomb. Metal or glass objects should not be used for shielding, for they will worsen the effects of the bomb if it should go off.
3. Mark off a danger zone that is at least three hundred feet in all directions from the bomb. This includes areas above and below it.
4. Open all doors and windows, if possible. This reduces damage from the blast and lessens the danger of flying glass.
5. Turn off, if possible, all gas and fuel lines at the main switches. Electrical equipment should also be turned off.

People are becoming extremely conscious of bombs. When *Skeptic* magazine was preparing its issue on terrorism, it had first hand experience with this. Artist David Jarvis, in preparing that month's cover illustration, had made a fake contraption of red tubes marked "dynamite" and an alarm clock, to use as a model. When he was finished, he slipped the contraption under his drawing board. It was found that night by a cleaning crew, who called the Los Angeles Police Department.

Kidnapping has become a favorite terrorist tactic. Businessmen, diplomats, and military personnel living abroad have taken steps to combat this. Since the kidnapping of Patricia Hearst by the Symbionese Liberation Army, prominent Americans are conscious of the threat and taking sensible precautions. These involve maintaining a low profile. This means keeping names, addresses, and photographs of family members out of newspapers. Some people are even dropping their listings in *Who's Who* and other directories. Photographs of company executives are being removed from offices and omitted from company publications. Care is taken not to announce travel plans in advance.

All potential kidnap victims, most especially those living overseas, are urged to vary their routines by traveling to and from home and office at different times or by going out to lunch and dinner at irregular hours. A sensible precaution is to take a different route to and from work each day. All such measures reduce the chance of kidnapping.

To protect American diplomats abroad, the federal government has increased the number of armed marines stationed in embassies and consulates. They accompany diplomats when they travel. Private corporations are now hiring bodyguards for overseas executives. Chauffeur and private drivers are being taught special motoring techniques to avoid kidnappers, such as throwing a car into a skid to reverse directions in a narrow space.

Police departments had other law-enforcement agencies have taken steps to combat terrorism. Intelligence activities have been greatly increased. Records are maintained, often being computerized, on known or suspected terrorists, revolutionaries, and subversives. Their activities are monitored and an effort is made to know their whereabouts at all times. Whenever possible, terrorist groups are infiltrated or information is obtained about them from paid spies. All this intelligence is now exchanged routinely on an international basis, so a theft of arms or a shipment of explosives or the sudden departure of a suspected terrorist signals a worldwide police alert.

These efforts are thought to have had some success. It was through intelligence that terrorists armed with Russian hand-held SAM-7 missiles were caught at the edge of the airport in Rome before they could destroy their intended Israeli airlines target. European airports have several times gone on the alert because intelligence indicated an attack was imminent. These efforts have doubtless thwarted many attempts. Surveillance and intelligence operations also keep terrorists off balance and on the run. If hurried by la-enforcement agencies, forced to move often and to keep in hiding, terrorists are put on the defensive and are less able to take the offensive with an attack.

Most experts on antiterrorism believe these intelligence activities must be greatly increased and extended to those countries which now offer safe havens to terrorists.

Police agencies have also developed techniques for dealing with terrorists who seize a building and hold hostages inside. The usual terrorist tactic is to threaten to kill the hostages unless their demands, such as releasing other terrorists in prison, are met. They usually also want an airplane provided and a guarantee of their safe conduct out of the country.

Law-enforcement agencies have learned to use restraint and patience in these cases. They surround the building and lay siege to it. The terrorists are not so much holding the building as being trapped inside it. The police employ a variety of tactics aimed at inducing the terrorists to realize that their situation is hopeless so they will release their hostages unharmed and surrender.

The government of Ireland used these tactics in a classic manner in the kidnapping of Dr. Tiede Herrema. After he and his two IRA abductors, a young man and woman, were located via the house-to-house search, police and troops surrounded the building. Dr. Herrema was being held on the second floor of a private dwelling. Police held the first floor and were stationed on the roof and all around the building. The siege continued day and night, with searchlights playing on the building to prevent an escape at night. The kidnappers wanted the release of an IRA prisoner held in a Dublin prison. The Irish authorities flatly refused to do this or to negotiate anything If Dr. herrema was released unharmed and the kidnappers surrendered, they would be given safe conduct to prison and a fair trial. Those were the government's terms, and the officials refused to budge from them.

The siege went on for three long midwinter weeks. Authorities kept in constant touch with the kidnappers, hollering to them up the stairwell from the first floor. Attempts were made to enter through the roof and via a ladder raised to a rear window. Both attempts were thwarted by the kidnappers. Apparently neither attempt was serious, but meant only as harassment.

Food, drink, towels, and other necessities were given to the besieged trio, but only in minimal quantities. Authorities wanted fatigue, hunger, and the futility of their situation to take its toll on the kidnappers. Inside the building, Dr. Herrema's quiet courage also was effective in helping the abductors see how immature, frightened, and foolish they were. It took a long time, but it worked. The kidnappers cracked, threw out their weapons, released Dr. herrema, and then surrendered. The world applauded the conduct of the Irish police, for if they had tried to storm the building, Dr. Herrema would surely have been killed.

The seizure of a suburban passenger train in Holland by seven South Moluccans provided another example of how authorities have learned to deal with such cases. The heavily armed terrorists stopped the train on a lonely stretch of tack in the Dutch countryside by pulling the emergency cord. When the engineer ran back to see why the train had been stopped, he was shot, becoming the first casualty. In ensuing days, two of the passengers were executed as proof the terrorists were serious about their threat to murder all the passengers. The gunmen thought they had killed a fourth passenger, but miraculously all their bullets missed him. He rolled off the train, feigning death, then ran to safety.

The Dutch government had experience in dealing with similar hijackings, so the plan it put into effect was a model of patience and psychology. The train was surrounded by Dutch troops. There was no escape. The basic strategy was to make no deals whatsoever, offer nothing to the terrorists but make them ask, stall for time to induce fatigue, and try to instill friendship between the terrorists and the hostages. It took courage and discipline to stick to the plan, for it was bitter winter weather, and the passengers, many of them elderly, were suffering.

Almost two days elapsed before the authorities had any contact with the terrorists. Finally, they agreed to permit a field telephone to be sent aboard the train so communication could begin. The terrorists wanted independence for the South Moluccan Islands, former Dutch territory and now part of Indonesia. Making no deals on this was easy, for the Dutch had now power to grant the independence if they had wanted to. The terrorists then barked a long series of demands for supplies needed for themselves and the hostages. The authorities parted this to the barest minimum, food, water, blankets, medicines, and toilet paper- and not very much of those.

Such stinginess had three purposes. One was to cause fatigue and hunger among the terrorists. The second was to cast the terrorists in the role of begging for supplies rather than demanding them. The third was to foster friendship between the hostages and the gunmen. This may have seemed incredible, but the Dutch believed it could happen if hostages and terrorists alike were made angry at the authorities for being so cheap and cruel.

It took thirteen cold days. But the plan worked. The terrorists grew tired, nervous, and jumpy. Their demands for food and supplies changed in tone to piteous begging. The terrorists began to feel sorry for the passengers. The leader even wept in remorse for having killed the passengers. Ultimately an accident happened. The terrorist leader, firing his gun into the ceiling of the train, was cut in the eye by metal fragments. He left the train, surrendering, to get medical treatment. The remaining terrorists held out a day or two longer, then also surrendered, their exercise having been entirely futile. These tactics did not work, however, in May-June, 1977, when South Moluccans seized another train and school.

Police, government officials, and ordinary citizens are learning to combat terrorism. An orderly society maybe menaced by extremist but it is not defenseless. Yet, these defensive measures are a stopgap. They leave the way open for terrorists to attempt new, perhaps more terrifying initiatives. Governments, including the United States, face some difficult problems in dealing with these threats. We consider these matters next.

14

Terrorism: Tactics, Targets and Technologies

All terrorist groups seek targets that are rewarding from their point of view and employ tactics that are consonant with their overriding political aims. Whereas left-wing terrorists like the German RAF and Italian RB have selectively kidnapped and assassinated persons whom they blamed for economic exploitation or political repression in order to attract publicity and promote a Marxist-Leninist revolution, terrorists motivated by a religious imperative have engaged in more indiscriminate acts of violence, directed against a few wider category of targets encompassing not merely their declared enemies, but anyone who does not share their religious faith. The actions of ethno-nationalist/separatist groups arguably fall somewhere in between these two models. On the one hand, the violent campaigns waged by groups like the PLO, the IRA and the Basque separatist organization ETA have frequently been more destructive and have caused far greater casualties than those of their left-wing counterparts. But, on the other, their violence has largely been restricted to a specifically defined 'target set': namely, the members of a specific rival or dominant ethno-nationalist group. Perhaps the lest consequential of all these terrorist group categories (in terms both of frequency of incidents and of impact on public and governmental attitudes) has been the disparate collection of recycled Nazis, racist 'political punk rocker' and other extreme right-wing elements that has sporadic and uncoordinated, seemingly mindless violence – fuelled as much by beer and bravado as by a discernible political agenda – is neither completely random nor unthinkingly indiscriminate. Indeed, for all these categories, the point is less their inherent differences than the fact that their tactical and targeting choices correspond to, and are determined by, their respective ideologies and attendant mechanisms of legitimization and justification; and, perhaps most critically, by their relationship with the intended audience of their violent acts.

The overriding tactical – and, indeed ethical – imperative for left-wing terrorists, for example, has been the deliberate tailoring of their violent acts to appeal to their perceived 'constituencies'. In a 1978 interview, the German left-wing terrorist Michael 'Bommi' Baumann denounced the hijacking of a Lufthansa passenger plane the previous year by terrorists seeking the release of imprisoned RAF members as 'madness … you can't take your life and place it above that of children and Majorca holiday-makers and say: *My* life is valuable! That is elitarian madness, bordering of Fascism.' For Baumann, the deliberate involvement of innocent civilians in that terrorist operation was not only counterproductive, but wrong. It was counterproductive in that it tarnished the left-wing terrorists' image as a true 'revolutionary vanguard' – using violence to draw attention to themselves and their cause and 'educate' the public about what the terrorists perceived as the inequities of the democratic-capitalist state. It was also wrong in itself because innocent persons–no matter what the political justification – should not be the victims of terrorist acts directed against the state.

For this reason, left-wing terrorists' use of violence historically has been heavily constrained. Their self-styled crusade for social justice is typically directed against governmental or commercial institutions, or specific individuals who they believe represent capitalist exploitation and repression. They are there fore careful not to undertake actions that might alienate potential supporters or their perceived constituency. Accordingly, left-wing violence tends to be highly discriminate, selective and limited. Individuals epitomizing the focus of the terrorists' ideological hostility – wealthy industrialists like Hans Martin Schleyer (who was kidnapped and later murdered by the RAF in 1977) or leading parliamentarians like Aldo Moro (who similarly was kidnapped and subsequently murdered by the RB) – are deliberately selected and meticulously targeted for their intrinsic 'symbolic' value. 'You know that we did not kidnap Moro the man, but [rather] his function,' explained Mario Moretti, the leader of the RB Rome column who masterminded the operation, during his trial in November 1984. For Moretti, Moro was first and foremost a powerful symbol: a former prime minister and reigning Christian Democratic Party chief; a political wheeler-dealer *par excellence* and architect of the impending historic compromise with the Italian Communist Party that would fundamentally alter the country's political landscape and further marginalize the RB. He was, in the terrorists' eyes, the 'supreme manager of power in Italy' for the previous twenty years, a man whom Moretti described as the 'demiurge of bourgeois power'. By abducting so important a leader and so profound a symbol, the RB sought to galvanize the Italian left and thereby decisively transform the political situation in their favor.

Even when less discriminate tactics such as bombing are employed, the violence is meant to be equally 'symbolic'. That is while the damage inflicted is real, the terrorists' main purpose is not to destroy property or obliterate tangible assets, but to dramatize or call attention to a political cause. The decision-making process of the left-wing terrorist group is perhaps depicted most clearly in Baumann's description of the planning of a 1969 terrorist attack by the group known as the Tupamaros West Berlin (a precursor of both the Second of June Movement and the original RAF). Baumann and his colleagues wanted to stage an operation that would simultaneously attract attention to themselves and their cause, publicize the plight of the Palestinian people and demonstrate the West German left's solidarity and sympathy with the Palestinians' struggle 'We sat down and pondered what would be a story that nobody could miss, that everyone would have to talk about and everyone would have to report,; Baumann recalled. 'And we came up with the right answer – a bomb in the Jewish Community Centre – and on the anniversary of the "Crystal Night" during the Third Reich ... Though it didn't explode, the story [still] went round the world.' By striking on this particular date, against this specific target, with its deep – and unmistakable – symbolic significance, the group sought to draw a deliberate parallel between Israeli oppression of the Palestinians and Nazi persecution of the Jews.

The use by left-wing terrorists of 'armed propaganda' (i.e. violent acts with clear symbolic content) is thus a critical element in their operational calculus. It is also the principal means by which these organizations 'educate' the masses thought their self-anointed role as 'revolutionary vanguard'. The first official 'strategic resolution' of the RB, for example, stressed this theme. 'It is not a question of organizing the class movement within the area of armed struggle,' the 1975 document sated, 'but of entrenching the organization of the armed struggle and the political realization of tis historical necessity within the class movement.' A less turgid explanation of this strategy was later offered by Patrizio Peci, leader of the group's Turin column, when he reflected how, 'As crazy as it might seem, the plan in a few words was this: First phase, armed propaganda ... Second phase, that of armed support ... Third phase, the civil war and victory. In essence, we were the embryo, the skeleton of the future ... the ruling class of tomorrow in a communist society.' The RAF drew similar parallels in its exegesis of the relationship between the terrorist vanguard and 'the people'. Our original conception of organization implied a connection between the urban guerrilla and the work at the base', explained the document entitled 'Sur las Conception de las Guerilla Urbaine';

> We would like it if each and all of us could work at the neighborhoods and factories, in socialist groups that already exist, influence discussion, experience and learn. This has proved impossible ...
>
> Some say that the possibilities for agitation, propaganda, and organization are far from being eradicated and that only when they are, should we pose the question of arms. We say: it will not really be possible to profit from any political actions as long as armed struggle does not appear clearly as the goal of the politicisation.

This approach is not entries dissimilar to that of many ethno-nationalist/separatist groups. These terrorist movements also see themselves as a revolutionary vanguard – if not in classics Marxist-Leninist terms, at least as a spearhead, similarly using violence to 'educate' fellow members of their nation or ethnic group about the inequities imposed upon them by the ruling government and the need for communal resistance and rebellion. As one Basque nationalist bluntly told and interviewer, 'ETA is the vanguard of our revolution.' Accordingly, like all ethno-nationalist/separatist terrorists, ETA uses demonstratively symbolic acts of violence to generate publicity and rally support by underscoring the powerlessness of the government to withstand the nationalist expression they campion, and thereby to embarrass and coerce it into acceding to the group's irredentist demands. Their 'target audience', however, is not just the local, indigenous population but often the international community as well. These groups, accordingly, recognize the need to tightly control and focus their operations in such a manner as to ensure both the continued support of their local 'constituencies' and the sympathy of the international community. What this essentially means is that their violence must always be perceived as both purposeful and deliberate, sustained and omnipresent. Gerry Adams himself expressed precisely this point in an article he wrote in 1976 to commemorate the sixtieth anniversary of the 1916 Easter Uprising.

Indeed, as the veteran Northern Ireland correspondent David McKittrick points out, 'Sinn Fein in its efforts to build a political machine in both parts of Ireland, has [always] been concerned to project IRA violence as the clinical and carefully directed use of force.'

The more successful ethno-nationalist/separatist terrorist organization will be able to determine an effective level of violence that is at once 'tolerable' for the local populace, tacitly acceptable to international opinion and sufficiently modulated not to provoke massive governmental crackdown and reaction. The IRA has demonstrably mastered this synchronization of tactics to strategy. Since the mid-1980s, according to Patrick Bishop and Eamonn Mallie, the organization's military high command has clearly recognized that 'Republican strategy required a certain level of violence - but only enough to distort the private and public life of the North, and to make sure that military arm was properly exercised. What this has often resulted in is the targeting of members of the security forces (ordinary policemen and soldiers) in preference to the terrorists' avowed enemies in some rival indigenous community. This is true in Northern Ireland, where fewer than 20 per cent of the IRA's victims between 1969 and 1993 were Protestant civilians, and in Spain, where more than 60 per cent of fatalities inflicted by the Basque ETA have been members of the Spanish security forces.

Certainly, 'traitors', informants, and other collaborators among their own brethren are regularly targeted; but here the terrorist group must be careful to strike another balance between salutary, if sporadic, 'lessons' that effectively intimidate and compel compliance from their own communities and more frequent and heavy-handed episodes that alienate popular support, encourage cooperation with the security forces and therefore prove counterproductive. By the same token, highly placed government officials and security force commanders will when the opportunity presents itself and the political conditions are propitious, be attacked. But given the combination of uncertain-and possibly undesirable - political and security repercussions, the difficulties involved in gaining access to these VIPs and the considerable effort required of such operations, they are generally eschewed in favor of more productive, if less spectacular, operations that, moreover, conform to the terrorists' perceptions of what are regarded as 'legitimate' or 'acceptable' targets - however abhorrent the attacks may seem to the outside world.

The terrorist campaign is like a shark in the water: it must keep moving forward- no matter how slowly or incrementally- or die. Hence, when these more 'typical' targets fail to sustain the momentum of a terrorist campaign, or when other, perhaps even totally unrelated events overshadow the terrorists and shunt their cause out of the public eye, terrorists often have to resort to more violent and dramatic acts to refocus attention back upon themselves. But is would be a mistake to see these acts - which often involve the bombing of public gathering-places or the hijacking of airliners - as random or senseless. For example, we saw in chapter 3 how, following the Palestinian terrorists' failure to mount a concerted guerrilla campaign against Israel in the occupied West Bank and Gaza Strip after the 1967 Six Day War, the PFLP began hijacking international airliners. The purpose of these operations was not wantonly to kill or otherwise harm innocent persons (in contrast to many subsequent terrorists' targeting of civil aviation) but to use the passengers as pawns in pursuit of publicity and the extraction of concession from unsympathetic governments.

Even when the terrorists' actions are not as deliberate or discriminating, and when their purpose is in fact to kill innocent civilians, the target is still regarded as 'justified' because it represents the terrorists' defined 'enemy'. Although incidents maybe quantitatively different in the volume of death or destruction caused, they are still qualitatively identical in that a widely known 'enemy' is being specifically targeted. This distinction is often accepted by the terrorists' constituents and at times by the international community as well. The recognition that the Palestinians obtained in the wake of the 1972 Munich Olympics massacre is a particularly prominent case in point. The poignant message left behind by the terrorist team struck precisely the sympathetic chord they had intended: 'We are neither killers not bandits,' their letter stated. 'We are persecuted people who have no land and no homeland ... We are not against any people, but why should our place here be taken by the flag of the occupiers ... why should the whole world be having fun and entertainment while we suffer with all ears deaf to us? As the PFLP's Bassam Abu Sharif explained, 'For violence to become fruitful, for it to get us to our aims, it should not be undertaken without a proper political base and intention.' While the logic in such a case my well be contrived, there is nonetheless a clear appreciation both that violence has its limits and that, if used properly, it can pay vast dividends. In other words, the level of violence must be kept within the bounds of what the terrorists' 'target audience' will accept.

But acts of terrorism, like battles in conventional wars, are difficult to limit and control once they started, and often result in tragedy to civilians who are inadvertently caught up in the violence. On well-known example is the tragic bombing that occurred at Enniskillen, Northern Ireland, in November 1987, causing the deaths of eleven innocent bystanders attending a memorial ceremony and injuries to sixty-three others. The IRA was quick to describe the incident as an accident resulting from the 'catastrophic consequences' of an operation against British troops gone away. In this instance, there was an acceptance that some grievous wrong had been done, albeit clothed in layers of self-serving justifications.

The Basque ETA is no different: alternately threatening and remorseful in communiques that seek to absolve itself of responsibility for its violent deeds and simultaneously to reap the rewards of introspection and self-criticism. 'We claim responsibility for the failed action against a member of the Spanish police,' reads once, 'following the placing of an explosive charge under his car. We very much deplore the accidental injuries involuntarily caused to his neighbor... and we wish his prompt and complete recovery.

Right-wing terrorism has often been characterized as the least discriminating, most senseless type of contemporary political violence. It has earned this reputation mostly as a result of the seemingly mindless 'street' violence and unsophisticated attacks that in recent years have increasingly targeted immigrants, refugees, guest workers and other foreigners in many European countries, especially in eastern Germany and other former communist-block states, but also from an inchoate bombing campaign that briefly convulsed Western Europe in the early 1980s. If the means of the right-wing terrorists sometimes appear haphazardly planned and often spontaneously generated, their ends are hardly less indistinct. Essentially, their ostensible goal is the destruction of the liberal-democratic state to clear the way for a renascent National Socialist ('Nazi') or fascist one. But the extent to which this is simply an excuse for the egocentric pleasure derived from brawling and bombing, preening or parading in 1940s-era Nazi regalia is hard to judge, given that the majority of right-wing groups do not espouse any specific program of reform, preferring to hide behind vague slogans of strident nationalism, the need for racial purity and the re-assertion of governmental strength. In sum, the democratic state is somewhat reflexively assailed for its antifold weaknesses - notably in liberal social welfare policies and tolerance of diverse opinion - alongside its permitting of dark-skinned immigrants in the national labor force and of Jews and other minorities in positions of power or influence. The right-wing terrorists believe that their nation's survival is dependent upon the exorcism of these elements from its environs; only by becoming politically, racially and culturally homogenous can the state recover its strength and again work for its natural citizens rather than the variegated collection of interlopers and parasites who now sap the nation of its strength and greatness.

It should be noted that, while the European groups share many similarities (racism, anti-semitism, xenophobia and a hatred of liberal government) with their American counterparts, they differ fundamentally in their mechanisms of legitimization and justification. Whereas the US groups may be more accurately categorized as religious - rather than strictly as right-wing terrorists because of the pivotal roles that liturgy, divine, inferences and clerical sanction play in underpinning and motivating their violence, the foundations of the European right are avowedly secular, with neither theological imperatives nor clerics exerting any significant influence. Indeed, the ill-defined, amorphous contours of the contemporary European extreme right's political philosophy can be summed up by the refrain from a popular song by the British white power band 'White Noise': 'Two pints of larger and a packet of crisps. Wogs out! White Power! or the folk song composed by Gottfried Kussel, Fuhrer of an Austrian neo-Nazi organization: 'Do you see his nose, no? Do you know his nose? His nose you do not know? It is crooked and ugly? Then hit him in the face. He is a Jew, a damned Jew, bloodsucker of the European race.' By comparison the lunatic and far-fetched millenarian views of American Christian white supremacists appear as deeply profound theological treaties.

It is for this reason, perhaps, that European right-wing terrorism has rarely transcended the boundaries of street brawls or the crude Molotov cocktail hurriedly tossed into a refugee shelter or a guest workers' dormitory (even though, of course, such crude acts of violence possess just the same tragic potential to kill and maim as much more sophisticated terrorist operations. Nonetheless, it would be a mistake to see right-wing violence as completely indiscriminate or entirely irrational. Indeed, the few occasions on which the neo-Nazis have attempted more ambitious types of operations have sent shock waves throughout the continent. In August 1980, for instance, a powerful explosion tore through the crowded rail station in Bologna, Italy, in the midst of the summer holiday crush. At the time, the total of eighty-four persons killed (and 180 wounded) was second only to the record ninety-one who had perished in a single terrorist act in the Irgun's bombing of the King David Hotel thirty-four years before. When it was followed less than a month later by a bombing at the popular Munich Oktoberfest celebration, killing fourteen and injuring another 215, fears were raised of a new terrorist onslaught more lethal and indiscriminate than that waged by either the European leftist terrorist organizations or the continent's various ethno-nationalist/separatist groups. But it did not materialize. Instead, the pattern of right-wing terrorism in Europe has remained largely the same since 1970s: one of sporadic attacks, alibiing specifically directed against particular types of targets – primarily refugee shelters and immigrant workers' hostels, anarchist houses and political party offices, and Arab and African immigrants walking along the street, as well as Jewish-owned property or business.

Crude and relatively unsophisticated and indeed intellectually depraved as this terrorist category may appear, then, like all forms of terrorism even right right-wing violence is not based on some pathological obsession to kill or beat up as many people as possible, but rather on a deliberate policy of intimidating the general public into acceding to specific demands or pressures. The right-wing terrorists see themselves, if not as a revolutionary vanguard than as a catalyst of events that will lead to the imposition of an authoritarian form of government. Thus, like other terrorist movements, they too tailor their violence to appeal to their perceived constituency - be it fellow extreme nationalists, intransigent racists and xenophobes, reactionary conservatives or militant anti-communists - and, with the exception of a handful of noteworthy, buy isolated, indiscriminate bombings, they seek to keep the violence they commit within the bounds of what the ruling government will tolerate without undertaking massive repressive actions against the terrorists themselves.

Moreover, the phenomenon by which terrorists consciously learn from one another, discussed in chapter 2, is evident in respect of at least some German right-wing terrorist elements. This suggests aspirations towards a more planned and coherent campaign of violence than has existed hitherto, raising the possibility of a more serious future threat. As long ago as 1981, Manfred Roeder, for a time Germany's leading neo-Nazi, advocated the emulation of left-wing terrorist targeting and tactics in hopes of endowing the movement with a clearer purpose and attainable goal. For the rightists, however, there was another factor: envy of the attention, status and occasional tactical victories won by left-wing terrorists in groups such as the RAF, alongside the realization that indiscriminate terrorist attacks would not result in the attainment of the neo-Nazis' goals. 'The RAF had brought terrorism to modern Europe,' Ingo Hasselbach, one of Roeder's successors, recently recalled, 'and even though they could not have been more opposed to our ideology, we respected them for their fanaticism and skill.' Hasselback therefore advocated for his *Kaeradschaft* (Nazi 'brotherhood'), before his own disillusionment forced him to break completely with the movement he had once so enthusiastically championed, a lethally discriminate campaign of terrorism mirroring that pursued by the RAF. Like the original founders of the Baader-Meinhof Group twenty years before, Hasselback also believed that his National Alternative Berlin (NA) neo-Nazi organization could not achieve its political objectives by attempting to operate as a legal political party. Accordingly he sought to mould the group into a terrorist organization modelled on the RAF and laid plans to assassinate prominent Jews and communists and leading politicians. 'We wanted to bring neo-Nazi terrorism up to the level of that carried out by the radical Left,' Hasselbach later explained, striking at targets that would be both better guarded and more significant – targets that would do serious damage to the democratic German state while driving home our racial message. There was, for instance, talk of assassinating Gregon Gusi, the head of the reformed Communist Party, the PDS; he was East Germany's most prominent Jew and leader of the Communists to boot. He was not only a major politician but the political representative of the former GDR system. We also considered hitting Ignatz Bubis, the new head of the Jewish community, as well as a number of politician in Bonn – including the interior minister and Chancellor Kohl himself.

Like other terrorist organizations, the more sophisticated right-wing groups also seek targets that are likely to advance their cause. In this respect, their terrorist acts are as calculated as those of the left-wing organizations they try to emulate. Publicity and attention are of course paramount aims; but at the same time there is a conscious recognition that only if their violence is properly calculated and at least in some (however idiosyncratic) way regulated, will they be able to achieve the effect(s) they desire and the political objectives they seek. As an IRA terrorist once said, 'You don't bloody well kill people for the sake of killing them.' This is not, however, the case with many of the religious terrorist movements discussed in chapter 4. For them, violence still has an instrumental purpose but, unlike secular terrorists, it is also often an end in itself – a sacred duty executed in direct response to some theological demand or imperative. A 1990 study of Lebanese Shi'a terrorists, for example, revealed that none of the sample was interested in influencing an actual or self-perceived constituency or in swaying popular opinion: their sole preoccupation was serving God through the fulfillment of their divinely ordained mission. Hence, for religious terrorists there are demonstrably fewer constraints on the actual infliction of violence and the category of targets/enemies is much more open-ended. The leader of an Egyptian terrorist cell, for instance, professed absolutely no remorse when he was told that an attack he had planned against visiting Israeli Jews had instead killed nine German tourists. His matter-of-fact response was that 'infidels are all the same'. Indeed, how else can one explain the mad plots of the American Christian while supremacists? Or the Aum sect's wanton and repeated attempts to use chemical warfare nerve agents indiscriminately in populous urban centres? Or the cataclysmic aim of the Jewish Temple Mount bomber in Israel? The willingness of religious terrorists to contemplate such wholesale acts of violence is a direct reflection of the fact that, their secular counterparts, they do not seek to appeal to any constituency or authority other than their own god or religious figures, and therefore feel little need to regulate or calibrate their violence.

The Organizational Dynamics of Terrorist Groups

All terrorists, however, have one trait in common: they live in the future, live for that distant – yet imperceptibly close – point in time when they will assuredly triumph over their enemies and attain the ultimate realization of their political destiny. For the religious groups, this future is divinely decreed and the terrorists themselves specifically anointed to achieve it. The inevitability of their victory is taken for granted, as a 1996 communique issued by the Egyptial Gamat al-Islamiya (Islamic Group) reveals. Citing the Qur'an, the document brusquely dismisses even the possibility that its secular opponents might succeed. 'They plot and plan and God too plans,' it declares, 'but the best of planners is God.' Therefore the group must faithfully and resolutely 'pursue its battle ... until such time as God would grant victory – just as the Prophet Mohammed did with the Quredish until God granted victory over Mecca.

For the secular terrorists, too, eventual victory is as inevitable as it is predetermined. Indeed, the innate righetousness of their cause itself assures success. 'Our struggle will be long and arduous because the enemy is powerful, well-organized, and well-sustained from abroad,' Leila Khaled wrote in her autobiography, published in 1973. 'We shall win because we represent the wave of the future... because making is on our side, and above all because we are determined to achieve victory.' Comparatively small in number, limited in capabilities, isolated from society and dwarfed by both the vast resources of their enemy and the enormity of their task, secular terrorists necessarily function in an inverted reality where existence is defined by the sought-after, ardently pursued future rather than the oppressive, angst-driven and incomplete present. 'You convince yourself that to reach this utopia', the Red Brigades' Adriana Faranda later recalled of the group's collective mindset, 'it is necessary to pass through the destruction of society which prevents your ideas from being realized.' By ignoring the present and literally 'soldiering on' despite hardship and adversity, terrorist are able to compensate for their abject weakness and thereby overcome the temporal apathy or hostility of a constituency whom they claim to represent. 'We made calculations,' Faranda's comrade-in-arms Patrizio Peci explained in his memoirs. 'The most pessimistic thought that within twenty years the war would be won, some said within five, ten. All, however, thought that we were living thought the most difficult moment, that gradually things would become easier.' The left-wing terrorists thus console themselves that the travails and isolation of life underground are but a mere transitory stage on the path to final victory.

The longevity of most modern terrorist groups, however, would suggest otherwise. Rapoport, for example, estimates that the life expectancy of at lest 90 per cent of terrorist organizations is less than a year, and that nearly half of those that make it as far as that have ceased to exist within a decade. Thus the optimistic clarion calls to battle issued by terrorist groups the world over in communiques, treatises and other propaganda have a distinctly hollow ring given the grim reality of their organizational life cycles. 'NEVER BE DETERRED BY THE ENORMOUS DIMENSIONS OF YOUR OWN GOALS' proclaimed a communique issued by the left-wing French terrorist group Direct Action in 1985: yet less than two years later the group had effectively been decapitated by the capture of virtually its entire leadership and shortly afterwards fell into complete lassitude. Similarly, in 1978 the RB leader, Renato Curio, bragged about a struggle that he envisioned would last forty years: but within a decade even this terrorist organization – for a time one of the 'Europe's most formidable – had collapsed under the weight of arrests and defections.

Some categories of terrorist groups admittedly have better chances of survival – and perhaps success – than others. Historically, although religious movements like the Assassins persisted for nearly two centuries and the Thugs remained active for more than six hundred years, in modern times ethno-nationalist/separatist terrorist groups have typically lasted the longest and been the most successful.

Al-Fatah, the Palestinian terrorist organization led by Yassir Arafat, for example, was founded in 1957. The PLO itself is now thirty-four years old. The Baswue group ETA was established in 1959, while the current incarnation of the IRA, formally known as the Provisional Irish Republican Army, is nearly thirty years old and is itself the successor of the older Official IRA that was founded nearly a century ago and can in turn be traced back to the various Fenian revolutionary brotherhoods that had surfaced periodically since Wolfe tone's rebellion in 1789. However, except in the immediate post-war era of massive decolonization, success for ethno-nationalist terrorist organizations has rarely involved the actual realization of their stated, long-term goals of self-determination or nationhood. More often it has amounted to a string of key tactical victories that have sustained prolonged struggle and breathed new life into faltering - and in some instances, geriatric - terrorist movements.

The resilience of these groups is doubtless a product of the relative ease with which they are able to draw sustenance and support from an existing constituency - namely, the fellow members of their ethno-nationalist group. By contrast, both left- and right-wing terrorist organizations must actively proselytize among the politically aware and radical, though often uncommitted, for recruits and support, thus rendering themselves vulnerable to penetration and compromise. The ethno-nationalist derive a further advantage from their historical longevity by being able to appeal collective revolutionary tradition and even at times a predisposition to rebellion. This assures successive terrorist generations both a steady stream of recruits from their respective communities' youth and a ready pool of sympathizers and supporters among their more nostalgic elders. These groups' unique ability to replenish their ranks from within already close, tightly knit communities means that even when a continuing campaign shows signs of flagging, the mantle can be smoothly passed to a new generation.

Abut Iyad, Arafat's intelligence chief, can therefore dismiss as mere emphemeral impediments the culs-de-sac and roundabouts that have long baulked the advance of the Palestinian liberation movement. 'Our people will bring forth a new revolution', he wrote some twenty years ago. 'They will engender a movement much more powerful than ours, better armed and thus more dangerous to the Zionists ... And one day, we will have a country.

The ethno-nationalists comparative success, however, may have as much to do with the clarity and tangibility of their envisioned future – the establishment (or reestablishment) of a national homeland from within some existing country – as to these other characteristics. The articulation of so concrete and comprehensible a goal is by far the most potent and persuasive rallying cry. It also makes the inevitable victory appear both palpable and readily attainable, even thought the path to it be prolonged and protracted. Few would have doubted Martin McGuinness's 1977 pledge that the IRA would keep 'battering on until Brits leave', or Danny Morrison's declaration twelve years later that 'when it is politically costly for the British to remain in Ireland, they'll go ... it won't be triggered until a large number of British soldiers are killed and that's what's going to happen'.

Left-wing terrorists movements by comparison, appear doubly disadvantaged. Not only do they lack the sizeable existing pool of potential recruits available to most ethno-nationalist groups, but among all the categories of terrorists they have formulated the least clear and most ill-defined vision of the future. Prolific and prodigious though their myriad denunciations of the evils of the militarist, capitalist state may be, precious little information is forthcoming about its envisioned successor. 'That is the most difficult question for revolutionaries.' Replied Kozo Okamoto, the surviving member of the three-man JRA team that staged the 1972 Lod Airport massacre, when asked about the post-revolutionary society that his group sought to create. 'We really do not know what it will be like.' The RAF's Gudrun Ensslin similarly brushed aside all questions about the group's long-term aims. 'As for the state of the future, the time after victory,' she once said, 'that is not our concern... we build the revolution, not the socialist model.' This inability to articulate coherently, much less cogently, their future plans may explain why the left-wing terrorists' campaigns have historically been the least effectual.

Even when left-wing terrorists have attempted to conceptualize a concrete vision of the future, their efforts have rarely produced anything more lucid or edifying than vebose disquisitions espousing an idiosyncratic interpretation of Marxist doctrine. 'We have applied the Marxist analysis and method to the contemporary scene - not transferred it, but actually applied it,' Ensslin wrote in a collection of RAF statements published by the group in 1977 (and subsequently banned by the German government). Yet no further elucidation of the desired result is offered, except the belief that Marxism will be rendered obsolete when the revolution triumphs and the 'capitalist system has been abolished'. Slightly more reflective is the exposition offered by the American radical Jane Alpert, who in her memoir explains how she and her comrades-in-arms believed that the world could be cleansed of all domination and submission, that perception itself could be purified of the division into subject and object, that power playing between nations, sexes, races, ages, between animals and humans, individuals and groups, could be brought to an end. Our revolution would create a universe in which all consciousness was cosmic, in which everyone would share the bliss we knew from acid [LSD], but untainted by fear, possessiveness, sickness, hunger, or the need for a drug to bring happiness.

Nonetheless, this vision comes across as so vague and idyllic as to appear almost completely divorced from reality: an effect, perhaps, of its drug-induced influence. That drugs played a part in the formulation of other leftist terrorist strategies is an interesting, though perhaps exaggerated, sidelight. Baumann, for example, also recounts the centrality of drugs to the would-be revolution. 'We said integrate dope into praxis too,' he recalled, 'no more separate shit, but a total unification around this thing, so that a new person in born out of the struggle. It should be noted, though, that a study commissioned by the Italian secret services in the 1970s discovered (somewhat counter intuitively) that right-wing terrorists were in fact more prone to base and indeed to use drugs than their left-wing counterparts. Two Italian psychiatrists conducting a related study attributed this tendency to the rightists' innate psychological instability, at least compared to Italian left-wing terrorists. 'In the right-wing terrorism', wrote Drs. Franco Ferracuti and Francesco Bruno, 'the individual terrorists are frequently psychopathological and the ideology is empty; in left-wing terrorism, ideology is outside of reality and terrorists are more normal and fanatical.

But it would be a grave error to dismiss the left-wing terrorists as either totally feckless and frivolous or completely devoid of introspection or seriousness of purpose. For them, the future was simply too large and abstract a concept to comprehend: instead, action - terrorist attacks specifically designed to effect the revolution - was embraced as a far more rewarding pursuit. Accordingly, it was Fanon, and not Marx, who arguably exerted the greater influence. For example, Susan Stern, a member of the 1970s-era American left-wing terrorist group, The Weathermen, recalled the dynamic tension between thought and action that permeated the group and affected all internal debate. 'Once we tore down capitalism, who would empty the garbage, and teach the children and who would decide that?' she and her comrades would often consider.

> Would the world be Communist? Would the Third World control it? Would all whites die? Would all

> sex perverts die? Who would run the prisons - would there be prisons? Endless questions like these were *raised* by the Weathermen, but we didn't have the answers. *And we were tired of trying to wait until we understood everything* [emphasis added].

The RAF'S seminal treatise, 'Sur la Conception de lad Guerilla Urbaine', reflects the same frustration. Quoting fellow revolutionary Eldridge Cleaver, a leader of the Black Panther Party, an African-American radical political organization active during the 1960s, it states: 'For centuries and generations we have contemplated and examined the shit from all sides. "Me, I'm convinced that most things which happen in this country don't need to be analyzed much longer", said Cleaver. The RAF put the words of Cleaver into practice.'

Indeed, all terrorists are driven by this burning impatience, coupled with an unswerving belief in the efficacy of violence. The future that they look forward to is neither temporal nor born of the natural progression of making: rather, is contrived and shaped, forged and moulded and ultimately determined and achieved by violence. 'What use was there in writing memoranda?'

> What value in speeches? ... No, there was no other way. If we did not fight we should be destroyed. To fight was the only way to salvation.
>
> When Descartes said: 'I think, therefore, I am,' he uttered a very profound thought. But there are times in the history of peoples when thought alone does not prove their existence ... There are times when everything in your cries out: your very self-respect as a human being lies in your resistance to evil.
>
> We fight, therefore we are!

Thirty years later, Leila Khaled similarly invoked the primacy of action over talk and bullets over words: 'We must act, not just talk and memorize the arguments against Zionism,' she counselled. This view was echoed by Yoyes, an ETA terrorist who lost faith in the endless promises that 'independence can be won by peaceful means. It's all a lie ... The only possibility we have of gaining our liberty is through violence.' As the former neo-nazi Ingo Hasselbach recalled of his own experience, 'The time for legal work and patience was through. The only thing to do was to turn our *Kameradschaft* into a real terrorist organization.'

For some terrorists, however, the desire for action can lead to an obsession with violence itself. Abu Nidal, for example, was once known and admired for his 'fiery and unbending nationalism', whereas today he is universally disdained as little more than an 'outlaw and killer'. Eamon Collins describes a similar transformation in his IRA-gunman cousin Mickey, who, Collins realized, had gradually 'lost any sense of the wider perspective, and was just obsessively absorbed by the details of the next killing'. Andreas Baader is perhaps a different type altogether. From the very start of the RAF's campaign, he never wavered from his conviction that the terrorist's only 'language is action'. Baumann, who knew Baader well, remembers the RAF's founder as a 'weapons maniac, [who] later developed an almost sexual relationship with pistols (the Heckler and Koch type in particular)'. Indeed, according to Baader himself, 'Fucking and shooting [were] the same thing.' Unquestionably a man of action and not words, he preferred, in the terrorist vernacular, 'direct actions' – bank robberies, vandalism and arson, bombings and armed attacks – to debate and discourse. 'Let's go, then!' was Baader's immediate response, for example, when his lover and co-leader Ensslin suggested that the group bomb an American military base in retaliation for the US air force's mining of the North Vietnam's Haiphong harbor in 1972. Despite being the leading figure of an organization dedicated to achieve profound political change, he had absolutely not time for politics, which he derisively dismissed as a load of 'shit'. Baader's whole approach can be summed up in the advice he gave to a wavering RAF recruit. 'Either you come along [and join the revolution and fight],' he said, 'or you stay forever an empty chatterbox.'

Although Baader may perhaps be an extreme example of this phenomenon, action is the undeniable cynosure for all terrorists - perhaps even more so, the thrill and heady excitement that accompany it. Far more of Peci's 222-page account of his life as a Red Brigadist, for instance is devoted to recounting in obsessive detail the types of weapons (and their technical specifications) used on particular RB operations and which group members actually did the shooting than to elucidating the organizations' ideological aims and political goals. Baumann is particularly candid about the cathartic relief that an operation brought to a small group of individuals living underground, in close proximity to one another, constantly on the run and fearful of arrest and betrayal. The real stress, he said, came from life in the group - not from the planning and execution of attacks. Others, like Stern, Collins, the RAF's Silke Maier-Witt and the RB's Susana Ronconi, are even more explicit about the 'rush' and the sense of power and accomplishment they derived from the violence they inflicted. 'Nothing in my life had ever been this exciting,' Stern enthused as she drifted deeper into terrorism. Collins similarly recalls how he led an 'action-packed existence' during his six years in the IRA, 'living each day with the excitement of feeling I was playing a part in taking on the Orange State'. For Maier-Witt, the intoxicating allure of action was sufficient to overcome the misgivings she had about the murder of Schleyer's four bodyguards in order to kidnap the man himself. 'At the time I felt the brutality of that action... [But it] was a kind of excitement too because something had happened. The real thing', she consoled herself, had 'started now'. Ronconi is the most expansive and incisive in analyzing the terrorist's psychology. 'The main thing was that you felt you were able to influence the world about you, instead of experiencing it passively,' thereby combining intrinsic excitement with profound satisfaction. 'It was this ability to make an impact on the reality of everyday life that was important,' she explained, 'and obviously still is important.'

For the terrorist, success in making this impact is most often measured in terms of the amount of publicity and attention received. Newsprint and air-time are thus the coin of the realm in the terrorists' mindset: the only tangible or empirical means they have by which to gauge their success and assess their progress. In this respect, little distinction or discrimination is made between good or bad publicity: the satisfaction of simply being noticed is often regarded as sufficient reward. 'The only way to achieve results,' boasted the JRA in is communique claiming credit for the 1972 Lod Airport massacre, in which twenty-six people were slain (including sixteen Puerto Rican Christians on a pilgrimage to the Holy land), 'is to shock the world right down to its socks.' The arch-terrorist Carlos 'The Jackal' reportedly meticulously clipped and had translated newspaper accounts about him and his deeds. 'The more I'm talked about,' Carlos once explained to his terrorist colleague – later turned apostate – Hans Joachim Klein, 'The more dangerous I appear. That's all the better for me.' Similarly, when Ramzi Ahmed Yousef, the alleged mastermind behind the 1993 bombing of New York's World Trade Center, was apprehended in Pakistan two years later, police found in his possession two remote-control explosive devices along with a collection of newspaper article detailing his exploits.

However, for Carlos and Yousef as for many other terrorists this equation of publicity and attention with success and self-gratification has the effect of locking them into an unrelenting upward spiral of violence in order to keep the eye of the media and the public on them. Yousef, for example, planned to follow the World Trade Center bombing with the assassinations of Pope John Paul II and the then prime minister of Pakistan Benazir Bhutto, and the near-simultaneous in-flight bombings of eleven US passenger airliners. Klein in fact describes escalation as a 'force of habit' among terrorists; an intrinsic product of their perennial need for validation which in turn is routinely assessed and appraised on the basis of media coverage. The effect is that terrorists today feel driven to undertake ever more dramatic and destructively lethal deeds in order to achieve the same effect that a less ambitious or bloody action may have had in the past. To their minds at least, the media and public have become progressively inured or desensitized to the seemingly endless litany of successive terrorist incidents; thus a continuous upward ratcheting of the violence is required in order to retain media and public interest and attention. As Klein once observed, the 'more violent things get, the more people will respect you. The greater the chance of achieving your demands.' Timothy McVeigh, the convicted Oklahoma City bomber, seemed to be offering the same explanation when responding to his attorney's question whether he could not have achieved the same effect of drawing attention to his grievances against the US government without killing anyone. 'That would not have gotten the point across,' McVeigh reportedly replied. 'We needed a body count to make our point.' In this respect, although the Murrah building bombing was doubtless planned well in advance of the portentously symbolic date of 19 April deliberately chosen by McVeigh, he may nonetheless have felt driven to surpass in terms of death and destruction the previous month's dramatic and more exotic nerve gas attack on the Tokyo underground in order to guarantee that his attack too received the requisite media coverage and public attention.

The terrorists' ability to attract – and, moreover, to continue to attract – attention is most often predicated on the success of their attacks. The most feared terrorists are arguably those who are the most successful in translating thought into action: ruthless and efficient, demonstrating that they are able to make good on their threats and back up their demands with violence. This organizational imperative to succeed, however, in turn imposes on some terrorist groups an operational conservatism that makes an ironic contrast with their political radicalism, decreeing that they adhere to an established *modus operandi* that, to their minds at least, minimizes the chances of failure and maximizes the chances of success. 'The main point is to select targets where success is 100% assured,' the doyen of modern international terrorism, George Habash, once explained. For the terrorist, therefore, a combination of solid training, sound planning, good intelligence and technological competence are the essential prerequisites for a successful operation. 'I learned how to be an effective IRA member,' Collins reminisced about his two-year training and induction period: 'how to gather intelligence, how to set up operations, how to avoid mistakes.'

Good intelligence, therefore, is as critical for the success of an operation as it is for the terrorists' own survival. An almost Darwinian principle of natural selection thus seems to affect terrorist organizations, whereby (as noted above) every new terrorist generation learns from its predecessors, becoming smarter, tougher and more difficult to capture or eliminate. In this respect, terrorists, also analyze the 'lessons' to be drawn from mistakes made by former comrades who have been either killed or apprehended. Press accounts, judicial indictments, courtroom testimony and trial transcripts are meticulously culled for information on security force tactics and methods and then absorbed by surviving group members. The third generation of the RAF that emerged in the late 1980s is a classic example of this phenomenon. According to a senior German official, group members routinely study 'every court case against them to discover their weak spots'. Having learned about the techniques used against them by the authorities from testimony presented by law enforcement personnel in open court (in some instances having been deliberately questioned on these matters by sympathetic attorney), the terrorists are consequently able to undertake the requisite countermeasures to avoid detection. For example, learning that the German police could usually obtain fingerprints from the bottom of toilet seats or the inside of refrigerators, surviving RAF members began to apply a special ointment to their fingers that, after drying, prevents fingerprints and thus thwarted their identification and incrimination. As a spokesperson for the Bundeskriminalamt (BKA or Federal Investigation Department) lamented in the months immediately preceding the RAF's unilateral declaration of a cease-fire in April 1992, the "Third Generation" learnt a lot from the mistakes of its predecessors – and bout how the police works ... they now know how to operate very carefully.' Indeed, according to a former member of the group, Peter-Jurgen Brock, now serving a life sentence for murder, the RAF before the cease-fire had 'reached maximum efficiency'.

Similar accolades have also been bestowed on the current generation of IRA fighters. At the end of his tour of duty in 1992 as General Officer Commanding British Forces in Northern Ireland, General Sir John Wilsey described the IRA as 'an absolutely formidable enemy. The essential attributes of their leaders are better than every before. Some of their operations are brilliant in terrorist terms.' By this time, too, even the IRA's once comparatively unsophisticated loyalist terrorist counterparts had absorbed the lessons of their own past mistakes and had consciously emulated the IRA to become disquietingly more 'professional' as well. One senior RUC officer noted this change in the loyalist terrorists' capabilities, observing that they too were now increasingly 'running their operations from small cells, on a need to know basis. They have cracked down on loose talk. They have learned how to destroy forensic evidence.

Technological Treadmill

"Finally, success for the terrorist is dependent on their ability to keep one step ahead not only of the authorities but also of counter terrorist technology". The terrorist group's fundamental organizational imperative to act also drives this persistent search for new ways to overcome or circumvent or defeat governmental security and counter-measures. The IRA's own relentless quest to pierce the armour protecting both the security forces in Northern Ireland and the most senior government officials in England illustrates the professional evolution and increasing operational sophistication of a terrorist group. The first generation of early 1970s IRA devices were often little more than crude anti-personnel bombs, consisting of a handful of roofing nails wrapped around a lump of plastic explosive and detonated simply by lighting a fuse. Time-bombs from the same era were hardly more sophisticated. Typically, they were constructed from a few sticks of dynamite and commercial detonators stolen from construction sites or rock quarries attached to ordinary battery-powered alarm clocks. Neither device was terribly reliable and often put the bomber at considerable risk. The process of placing and actually lighting the first type of device carried with it the potential to attract undesired attention while affording the bomber little time to effect the attack and make good his or her escape. Although the second type of device was designed to mitigate precisely this danger, its timing and detonation mechanism was often so crude that accidental or premature explosions were not infrequent, thus causing some terrorists inadvertently to kill themselves - what is known in Belfast as 'own goals'.

In hopes of obviating, or at lest reducing, these risks, the IRA's bomb-makers invented a means of detonating from a safe distance using the radio controls for model aircraft purchased at hobby shops. Scientists and engineers working in the scientific research and development division of the British Ministry of Defence (MoD) in turn developed a system of electronic countermeasures and jamming techniques for the army that effectively thwarted this means of attack. However, rather than abandon this tactic completely, the IRA began to search for a solution. In contrast to the state-of-the art laboratories, huge budgets and academic credentials of their government counterparts, the IRA's own 'R&D' department toiled in cellars beneath cross-border safe houses and the back rooms of urban tenements for five years before devising a network of sophisticated electronic switches for their bombs that would ignore or bypass the army's electronic countermeasures. Once again, the MoD scientists returned to their laboratories; emerging with a new system of electronic scanners able to detect radio emissions the moment the radio is switched on - and, critically, just tens of seconds before the bomber can actually transmit the detonation signal. The almost infinitesimal window of time provided by this 'early warning' of impending attack was just sufficient to allow army technicians to activate a series of additional electronic measures to neutralize the transmission signal and render detonation impossible.

For a time, this mechanism in its turn proved effective. But then the IRA discovered a means to outwit even this countermeasure. Using radar detectors like those used by motorists in the United States to evade speed traps, in 1991 the group's bomb-makers fabricated a detonating system that can be triggered by the same type of hand-held radar gun used by police throughout the world to catch speeding drivers. Since the radar gun can be aimed at its target before being switched on, and the signal that it transmits is nearly instantaneous, no practical means currently exists either to detect or to intercept the transmission signal. Moreover, shortly after making this breakthrough the IRA's 'R&D'

units developed yet another means to detonate bombs, using a photo-flash 'slave' unit that can be triggered from a distance of up to 800 meters by a flash of light. This device, which sells for between £60 and £70, is used by commercial photographers to produce simultaneous flashes during photo shoots. The IRA bombers attach the unit to the detonating system on a bomb and then simply activate it with an ordinary, commercially available, flash gun.

Not surprisingly, therefore, the IRA bombers have earned a reputation for their innovative expertise, adaptability and cunning. 'There are some very bright people around,' the British Army's Chief Ammunition Technical Officer (CATO) in Northern Ireland commented. 'I would rate them very highly improvisation. IRA bombs are very well made.' A similar accolade was offered by the staff officer of the British army's 321 Explosives and Ordnance Disposal Company: 'We are dealing with the first division,' he said. 'I don't think there is any organization in the world as cunning as the IRA.' They have had twenty years at it and they have learned from their experience. We have a great deal of respect for their skills ... not as individuals, but their skill.' While not yet nearly as good as the IRA, the province's loyalist terrorist groups have themselves been on a 'learning curve' with regard to bomb-making, and are said to have become increasingly adept in the construction, concealment and surreptitious placement of bombs.

In certain circumstances, even attacks that are not successful in conventionally understood military terms of casualties inflicted or assets destroyed can still be counted a success for the terrorists provided that they are technologically daring enough to garner media and public attention. Although the IRA failed to kill the prime minister, Margaret Thatcher, at the Conservative Party's 1984 conference in Brighton, the technological ingenuity of the attempt, involving the bomb's placement at the conference site weeks before the event and its detonation timing device powered by a computer microchip, nonetheless succeeded in capturing the world's headlines and providing the IRA with a platform from which to warn Mrs. Thatcher and all other British leaders: 'Today we were unlucky, but remember we only have to be lucky one–you will have to be lucky always.' Similarly, although the remote-control mortar attack staged by the IRA on No. 10 Downing Street as Mrs. Thatcher's successor John Major and his cabinet met at the height of the 1991 Gulf War failed to hit its intended target, it nonetheless successfully elbowed the war out of the limelight and shone renewed media attention on the terrorists, their cause and their impressive ability to strike at the nerve-centre of the British government even at a time of heightened security. 'The Provies are always that step ahead of you,' a senior RUC officer has commented. 'They are very innovative.' Although the technological mastery employed by the IRA is arguably unique among terrorist organizations, experience has nonetheless demonstrated repeatedly that, when confronted by new security measure, terrorists will seek to identify and exploit new vulnerabilities, adjusting their means of attack accordingly and often carrying on despite the obstacles placed in their path.

Conclusion

'All politics is a struggle for power,' wrote C. Wright Mills, and 'the ultimate kind of power is violence.' Terrorism is where politics and violence intersect in the hope of delivering power. All terrorism involves the quest for power: power to dominate and coerce, to intimidate and control, and ultimately to effect fundamental political change. Violence (or the threat of violence) is thus the *sine qua non* of terrorists, who are unswervingly convinced that only through violence can their cause triumph and their long-term political aims be attained. Terrorists therefore plan their operations in a manner that will shock, impress and intimidate, ensuring that their acts are sufficiently daring and violent to capture the attention of the media and, in turn, of the public and government as well. Often erroneously seen as indiscriminate or senseless, terrorism is actually a very deliberate and planned application of violence. It may be represented as a concatenation of five individual processes, designed to achieve, sequentially, the following key objectives:

1. *Attention.* Through dramatic, attention-riveting acts of violence, terrorists seek to focus attention on themselves and their causes through the publicity they receive, most often from news media coverage.
2. *Acknowledgment.* Having attracted this attention, and thrust some otherwise previously ignore or hitherto forgotten cause on to the state's–or, often more desirably, the international community's–agenda, terrorists seek to translate their new-found notoriety into acknowledgment (and perhaps even sympathy and support) of their cause.
3. *Recognition.* Terrorists attempt to capitalize on the interest and acknowledgment their violent acts have generated by obtaining recognition of their rights (i.e. acceptance of the justification of their cause) and of their particular organization as *the* spokesman of the constituency whom the terrorists purport to, or in some cases actually do, represent.
4. *Authority.* Armed with this recognition, terrorists seek the authority to effect the changes in government and/or society that lie at the heart of their movement's struggle: this may involve a change in government or in the entire state structure, or the redistribution of wealth, re-adjustment of geographical boundaries, assertion of minority rights, etc.
5. *Governance.* Having acquired authority, terrorists seek to consolidate their direct and complete control over the state, their homeland and/or their people.

While some terrorist movements have been successful in achieving the first three objectives, rarely in modern times has any group attained the latter two. Nonetheless, all terrorists exist and function in hopes of reaching this ultimate end. For them, the future rather than the present defines their reality. Indeed, they can console themselves that it was only a decade ago that the British prime minister, Margaret Thatcher, said the African National Congress, 'Anyone who thinks it is going to run the government in South Africa is living in cloud-cuckoo land.' Exactly ten years after that remark was uttered, Queen Elizabeth II greeted President Nelson Mandela on his first official state visit to London.

15

America's Bomb Culture

Some New Jersey teenagers fax two bomb threats to their high school in an alleged attempt to extort $1.3 million. In the home of one of them, police find a bomb making manual called *Jolly Roger's Cookbook,* which, they say, had been downloaded from the Internet. In Albuquerque, New Mexico, a live grenaded is found in a newspaper-vending box; a day later, police discover an 8-in. pipe bomb on a bridge. These incidents, which happened last week and caused no injury, may seem almost mundane compared to tragedy on the scale of the Oklahoma City blast and the notoriety of the Unabomber. Yet they represent a far more insidious danger: America's growing fascination and familiarity with bombs. In real life and in the movies, exploding devices have become commonplace. Joseph Grubisic, the commander of the Chicago police department's bomb squad, has seen an increase in bomb use by Cook County gangs and drug rings. His unit coined the term MacGyver bombs to identify a class of homemade devices he believes were inspired by the TV series. "We get a dozen or so a year," he says.

Grubisic's experience is reflected in the data collected by the FBI's Bomb Data Center, which counted 1,880 bombings in 1993, up from 442 a decade earlier. In 1993, bombs killed 43 and injured 281, up from 29 dead and 230 wounded two years earlier. The increase does not take into account the six deaths and 1,042 injuries caused by the 1993 bombing of the World Trade Center. According to the

Bureau of Alcohol, Tobacco and Firearms, about half the bombing attempts in 1993 were acts of vandalism, 13% were intended as revenge and fewer than 1% were acts of protest.

A significant factor in the increase in bombings is that the dissemination of bomb know-how has become a minor industry. The past few decades have produced the rise of mail-order publishing companies that serve the so-called gun aftermarket, including the gun fanciers, survivalists, wannabe cops and closet anarchists who like to shop for such products as laser sights, camouflage, fake badges and fake FBI and ATF hats. Some of their most popular offerings are "burn-and-blow" books that describe in detail how to make landmines, booby traps and bombs. "The information is available on the Internet and everywhere else," says retired ATF agent Al Gleason, who spent 50 years investigating bombings. "People who feel that the bomb might be their weapon of choice now have the information to make one."

One of the earliest and most successful products of these publishers is the *Anarchist Cookbook,* which was put out in 1971 by Lyle Stuart Inc. But to bomb-squad commanders, the most notorious publishers in Paladin Press in Boulder, Colorado, founded in 1970 by two Special Forces veterans of the Vietnam War. The company carries a catalog of 40 books and videos on how to make explosives, including the *Improvised Munitions Black Book* series-repackaged versions of military manuals with instructions for building explosives. Paladin's list also carries *Homemade C-4: A Recipe for Survival,* about which one catalog edition says, "Serious survivors know that the day may come when they need something more powerful than commercial dynamite ... For blowing bridges, shattering steel and derailing tanks, they need C-4."

Burn-and-blow publishers argue that there is no correlation between their material, which often carries the caveat "for information purposes only," and the increasing rate of bombings across the nation. "I sell a thousand books, but there ain't a thousand explosions," says Billy Blann, the owner of Delta Press Ltd. of El Dorado, Arkansas. The flurry of orders after the Oklahoma bombing for the pamphlet *Improvised Munitions from Ammonium Nitrate,* he says, is "just armchair people who want to know what's going on."

Hollywood too has become fascinated. With gunplay so common in real life, producers have turned to bombers as the villians du jour. On TV, the season finale of *Melrose Place* features a character who sets off a bomb at the apartment complex that houses the show's cast. The ABC soap opera *All My Children* contains a story line in which a character has been planning to bomb an ex-lover on his wedding day. In the wake of the Oklahoma bombing, producers of the soap opera say they are altering the bomb angle, while *Melrose Place's* producers are considering the same measure. At the movies, the new Chuck Norris film *Top Dog* begins with the bombing of an apartment building by neo-Nazis. Due May 19 is the Bruce Willis thriller *Die Hard with a Vengeance,* which opens with the bombing of a department store. Bombings have been featured in *Speed, Blown Away* and *The Specialist.* Moviemakers contend that they are merely reflecting reality. Says Graham Yost, the screenwriter for *Speed:* "We looked at bombings taking place all around the world and basically brought the conflict home to America." Tragically, real-life bombers maybe doing the same thing.

Connect the Dots

When the full history of home-grown American terrorism in the 1990's is written, the chapter before Oklahoma City will tell of a little-noticed press conference last August in New York.

It was called by Planned Parenthood to showcase a videotape of a meeting held by the Wisconsin branch of the far-right U.S. Taxpayers Party. The meeting's speakers, Randall Terry of Operation Rescue and Matthew Trewhella of Missionaries to the Preborn. But they weren't talking about abortion. Mr. Trewhella spoke of training his young child to use guns. The meeting's attendees were offered a manual titled "Principles Justifying the Arming and Organizing of a Militia" in which the Bible was invoked to justify the formation of "assault teams" to protect the unborn.

For Planned Parenthood, which had been forced by Reagan-era Federal indifference to do its own research into the steep 1980's rise in abortion-clinic bombings and murder, this demonstrable link between anti-abortion extremists and a growing militia movement was a major breakthrough. In the stepped-up investigation that followed, Planned Parenthood began to uncover a commingling of anti-abortion extremists, new-world-order paranoids, Waco wackos, Reconstructionist Christians, white supremacists and assault-weapon fanatics in a national paramilitary subculture. Abortion turned out to be merely the come-on issue, designed to attract followers to a rabid antigovernment crusade.

Since the Oklahoma bombing, Federal law enforcement officials have been in constant touch with Planned Parenthood, explained Pamela Maraldo, the organization's president. By now they've no doubt seen an anti-abortion terrorism manual from the mid-1980's with an elaborate illustrated plan for building a fertilizer bomb. Presumably the F.B.I. is also consulting the Southern Poverty Law Centre, the Anti-Defamation League and the American Jewish Committee, which, like Planned Parenthood, were driven by criminality in their own backyards to investigate the paramilitary right. As the Jewish weekly *The Forward* reported last week, anti-Semitic violence in the militia strongholds of Idaho and Montana is now routine.

It's not yet known whether this evidence will connect a specific militia or far-right group to the Oklahoma tragedy. What is clear is how extensively the nation's far-right factions are interconnected, forming a political network that often publicly espouses the same ideology as the terrorists in our midst, much as the Sinn Fein speaks aboveground for the I.R.A.

For one example of the far right's cohesiveness, consider Lawrence Pratt, head of the rabid Gun Owners of America. Wearing another had, Mr. Patt also runs the Committee to Protect the Family Foundation, a fund-raiser for Operation Rescue. As a public speaker, Mr. Pratt tours with "Preparedness Expo '95,' where he shares top billing with Mark ("from Michigan") Koernke, the shortwave radio voice of the militia movement, and Bo Gritz, the Idaho militia guru and Christian Covenant leader who last week described the Oklahoma bombing as "a Rembrandt—a masterpiece of science and art put together."

And who is the biggest recipient of campaign funds from Mr. Pratt's Gun Owners of America? None other than Representative Steve Stockman, the Texas Republican who last week denied any connection to militias when asked to explain the mysterious fax his office received after the Oklahoma bombing. Even so, *Roll Call,* the Capitol Hill paper, condemned Mr. Stockman and Idaho's Representative Helen Chenoweth on Thursday in an editorial titled "Paranoid Fringe."

At last, though at a high price, the country and Justice Department are starting to catch up to Planned Parenthood. As Frederick Clarkson, one of its researchers of the radical right, says: "Abortion clinics have had an average of 15 bombings or arsons every year for a decade. If that had happened at churches or newspapers or Federal office buildings, we would have called it terrorism. But society didn't want to recognize the pattern of violence."

Now that we're starting to recognize the complexity of that pattern, we also see that even when all the Oklahoma City bombing suspects are arrested, the investigation will have only just begun.

16

Anti-Terrorism: How Far?

Enemy Within

In the 1970s the nation allowed its domestic anti-terrorism apparatus to be crippled and virtually disbanded. Leading the destruction was a coalition of conscientious civil libertarians and radical revolutionaries dedicated to destroying constitutional government in the United States.

In 1971, the American Civil Liberties Union announced that "dissolution of the nation's vast surveillance network" would henceforth be a top priority. It launched a "police surveillance project" headed by Yale Law Professor Frank J. Donner, identified in sworn testimony by three witnesses as a steadfast member of the Communist Party in its worst Stalinist days. The National Lawyers Guild, whose president declared its goal was "to keep the road clear of legal roadblocks" for revolutionaries, filed law suits wholesale against local police intelligence units, crippling them or destroying them altogether. Old Left lawyer William Kunstler once boasted, "I stay in this profession only because I want to be a double agent, to destroy the whole … system.

The *Washington Post* and *New York Times* aided these crusades in both news and editorial columns. On December 22, 1974, the *Times* launched a major "expose" of the sins of American intelligence agencies on the domestic front. This "scoop" was based on an internal study of the CIA ordered by Director William Colby, in which subordinates were instructed to review the agency's 25-year history and report every activity that might have violated a domestic law. Colby naively handed the study over to *Times* reporter Seymour Hersh, and the newspaper treated it as a major scandal.

The U.S. Senate, meanwhile, created a select committee under the chairmanship of Frank Church (D., Idaho), the Senate's most intense left-wing ideologue. In March 1976, after more than a year of bombardment by Church and others on Capitol Hill, Attorney General Edward Levi, trying to position the weak Ford Administration for the approaching election imposed "guidelines" on the FBI prohibiting any investigation without "specific articulable facts giving reasons to believe that an individual or a group is or may be engaged in" criminal activities.

This requirement fro a "criminal predicate" totally abandoned law enforcement's preventive and peace-keeping functions. In the words of one jurist, "It means every terrorist gets one free blast." Five days before Levi issued his guidelines, the FBI's intelligence division had 4,868 domestic security investigations going. Six months later there were 626. By August 1982 Congress found the number had dwindled to 38.

The high cost of this destruction of domestic intelligence was demonstrated exactly a year after Attorney General Levi issued his guidelines. In Washington, D.C., a black Muslim guru named Hamaas Abdul Khaalis and 11 followers, wielding guns and machetes, seized hostages in the B'nai B'rith headquarters, the Muslim Mosque and Cultural Center, and the District of Columbia Building—Washington's "city hall." The Hanafi Muslims (as the cult called itself) killed one person and crippled another for life in their violent takeover. The siege lasted two days before the 137 hostages were released. The Metropolitan Police Department revealed that it had withdrawn an informant from the Hanafi Muslims and destroyed their filed, in response to pressure from the ACLU and other police baiters. The Senate Subcommittee on Criminal Laws and Procedures in a 1978 report asserted that if the police had an informer in the Hanafi ranks, "the chances are 100 to 1 that they would have had intelligence enabling them to take preventive action."

It was a different story in Maryland in 1978. State Police Sergeant John Cook infiltrated the Ku Klux Klan and fed the FBI reports on its violent plottings. The FBI opened a preliminary investigation under the Levi guidelines, but closed it when nothing had happened in 90 days, as the guidelines mandated. Fortunately, the Maryland State Police did not follow the FBI's lead. They kept Sergeant Cook in place, and he worked his way into a ten-man Klan "death squad." Eventually the Klan attempted a series of bombings, including one at the home of a black congressman, Parren Mitchell. The night of their planned attacks Sergeant Cook had the pleasure of arresting them.

Terror Network U.S.A.

On October 20, 1981, in Nyack, N.Y., a dozen Black Liberation Army and Weather Underground terrorists killed a Brank's guard, wounded two others, and made away with $1.6 million. At a police barricade five miles away they killed two cops and wounded a third. Four of the robbers were captured and the cash recovered, but eight or more escaped.

Tracing auto tags noted by witnesses, the FBI found several terrorist lairs. Seized documents showed the group was moving to a more vicious level of urban guerrilla warfare. A list profiled two dozen corporate executives and contained biographies, photos, and daily schedules of top New York and New Jersey police officials. Plots for bombings and ambush murders were evident in hand-drawn floor plans and photos of police stations and barracks. The terrorists also had a file on former President Nixon's residences. The evidence revealed a nationwide alliance of radical groups: the BLA, the Weather Underground, the Separatist Republic of New Afrika, the Puerto Rican FALN.

They even had links to radical feminists who ran a remote California commune where Sara Jane Moore engaged in target practice before her 1975 attempt to kill President Ford, and where the Symbionese Liberation Army kidnappers prepared their abduction of Patty Hearst and their murder of Oakland's black school superintendent, Marcus Foster. The allies had pulled off at least 18 "armed expropriations" with more than a million dollars in loot, and had freed notorious terrorists from prison. Incredibly, this Terror Network U.S.A. had operated for over five years without either police or FBI intelligence catching a hind in the connections. In those five years the FBI's informants in political-terrorist groups had been cut from 1,000 to fewer than 50, and its domestic security investigations from 20,868 to only 10 groups and 47 individuals.

The FBI had followed the Weather Underground from its beginning, when it spun off from the Students for a Democratic Society in 1969. The investigation continued after the 1976 Levi guidelines because the Weather terrorists had committed numerous bombings—including at the U.S. Capitol, the Pentagon, and some 18 other targets—prior to March 1974. But in October 1981 an FBI official admitted that "federal intelligence reports" were dropped in 1979 because the Weather gang "has not been active since it claimed responsibility for the 1977 bombing of a federal building in Seattle."

So unless a terrorist network announces itself periodically with press releases claiming credit for its bombings, the FBI will not chase it? That was the practice if not the disclosed rule—and continues almost so today. And the G-Men had good reasons to drop their pursuit of the Weather terrorists. Incredibly, the Carter Justice Department had more than two dozen lawyers and a grand jury investigating 132 FBI agents for alleged civil-rights violations of relatives and friends of fugitive terrorists, while non pursued the terrorists themselves.

In 1988, the anti-intelligence combine battered the FBI again just to keep the watchdogs intimidated. The Center for Constitutional Rights, founded in 1966 by Kunstler and three other Old Left lawyers, used the Freedom of Information Act to obtain from the FBI some 1,200 pages of files on the Committee in Solidarity with the People of El Salvador (CISPES).

The *New York Times* and *Washington Post* promptly disseminated the FBI's outrages. "FBI agents took photographs of marchers and recorded their automobile license numbers," *Times* reported Philip Shenon panted. "Agents were also authorized to begin surveillance of students at Florida State University." And the *Post's* Howard Kurtz seemed slack-jawed that "FBI agents investigated nuns, union members, and college students; checked up on church forums and Knights of Columbus dinners; photographed protestors at peaceful rallies; and distributed what they deemed offending articles for student newspapers and *People* magazine." Neither the *Post* not the *Times* gave its readers any hint of what had triggered the FBI probe—evidence indicating that CISPES militants might be sheltering the terrorists who had perpetrated the November 7, 1983, bombing of the U.S. Capitol.

Leon Trotsky, founder of the Red Army and one of the twentieth century's chief theoreticians and proponents of terrorism, proclaimed, "No terrorist group can function without a screen of sympathizers." CISPES clearly fit the definition of a terrorist screen. In May 1980 Fidel Castro ordered the various Marxist paramilitary factions warring against the Salvadoran government to form a unified command as the condition for greater East Bloc support. The new umbrella organizations—the military Farabundo Marti National Liberation Front (FMNL) and its political/diplomatic arm, the Revolutionary Democratic Front (FDR)—launched a program to build support inside the

United States. Shortly thereafter, conventions of leftists were held in Los Angeles and Washington, and CISPES was born.

In 1983 the FBI learned that individuals in contact with the FDR/FMLN planned to establish clandestine cells in the United States to commit murders, sabotage, and bank robberies in support of the Salvadoran guerrillas. On March 30 Headquarters authorized 11 field offices to investigate CISPES locally. Within a month, a bomb had exploded at the National War College in Washington, D.C. Numerous bombings followed – including the one at the U.S. Capitol – and anonymous "communiques" proclaimed solidarity with the Salvadoran insurgents.

CISPES members were the prime suspects until late March 1984. Then the FBI learned that some of the Nyack fugitives and their allies were responsible. However, as a result of its investigation, the FBI was able to head off the disruptive demonstrations CISPES was planning at the GOP convention in Dallas. The FBI continued its investigation until June 1985.

The entire CISPES investigation involved the equivalent of five full-time agents working over two years, and cost little more than $800,000. After the *Times* and *Post* horripilations the Justice Department's Office of Professional Responsibility and the FBI's inspection division spent almost that much investigating the CISPES investigation in order to mollify the Kunstlerites, the *Times,* the *Post,* and their congressional claque. The Senate Intelligence Committee faulted the Bureau for investigating the whole CISPES organization instead of a few specific suspects. But how was the FBI to know who the suspects were, or how extensive their network was, without looking? And who can say what mischief or mayhem the surveillance prevented – thereby coincidentally protecting the constitutional rights of the large majority of CISPES members to protest peacefully?

The current criminal-conduct only guidelines ignore the well-documented sociology of terrorist movements. Such movements contain only a few who will build and plant bombs, or lay and execute ambushes. But many will give the actors support: medical help, money, hiding places, intelligence, and such. These support networks must be built in advance of the onslaught. Building them requires worlds to attract and recruit sympathizers. This is the stage at which prevention is possible; and if prevention fails, swift apprehension can limit the damage.

Thus, in June 1970 an FBI informant within the Black Panther Party warned of a planned ambush on Detroit police, and named the designated attackers. On the appointed day two snipers riddled a police cruiser with armor-piercing bullets. Miraculously the two officers were only wounded. The killers were intercepted when they returned to their residence, and sent away for long prison terms. Three other named Panthers scouting another section of Detroit for a diversionary target were caught with illegal weapons and sent to jail as well.

Breaching the Screen

Penetrating the terrorist's screen of sympathizers requires intelligence of a surgical precision that can be obtained only with the full arsenal of clandestine operations: informant networks, electronic surveillance, covert action. An enlightening example is the first conviction under the Biological Weapons Anti-Terrorism Act of 1989.

On May 20, 1992, Colette Baker walked into the Pope County Sheriff's Office in Glenwood, Minnesota, and complained that her husband, Doug Baker, had pointed a shotgun at her and threatened to kill her. She wanted to leave him, she said, but feared he would kill her or her parents with a powerful poison that he had bragged of possessing. To persuade the skeptical cops, the next day

Mrs. Baker brought in a coffee can containing a baby-food jar, a finger-nail-polish bottle, a pair of rubber gloves, and a hand-printed note that read:

> "DOUG, Be extremely careful! After you mix the powder with the gel, the slightest contact will kill you! If you breathe the powder or get it in your eyes, you're a dead man. Dispose all instruments used. Always wear rubber gloves and then destroy them also.
>
> "Good hunting!!"
>
> "P.S. Destroy this note!!"
>
> A "smiley face" had been drawn next to the words, "Good hunting!!"

The FBI laboratory in Washington, D.C., found that the baby-food jar contained 0.7 gram of a castor-bean extract known as ricin, the third most deadly poison known. This tiny amount was enough to kill more than 100 people. Ricin has no antidote and is virtually impossible to detect in post-mortem analysis. (Ricin was the poison the KGB-controlled Bulgarian secret service used to murder Geogi Markov on a London street in 1978.)

The second bottle in Mrs. Baker's can contained a common skin-care product impregnated with dimethyl sulfoxide (DMSO), a powerful solvent that can transport toxic substances through the skin into the bloodstream in seconds.

This laboratory analysis was enough to get the FBI's concentrated attention. For more than a year local police had been passing along tipster' warnings about a shadowy group of tax protestors called the Patriots Council, meeting sporadically in various central-Minnesota towns such as ST. Cloud, Alexandria, Glenwood, and Starbuck. The group met on Sundays under guise of discussing religion, but there was hot talk against lawmen. One informant named three acquaintances who had discussed procuring assault rifles, killing a sheriff's deputy, and blowing up a federal building.

The FBI knew ricin was a favorite item in paranoid press. One sheet, published in Oregon, advertised ricin as the "Silent Tool of Justice ... agent of choice for CIA, KGB, etc. A single bean will kill an evildoer." Mrs. Baker's coffee can was just the lucky break the FBI needed to prevent what might have been a deadly disaster. This was preventive law enforcement at its best. The FBI went back to the sheriff's detectives who had been reporting on the Patriots Council and recruited one of the tipsters, Scott Loverink, as an informant. Over the next 14 months Loverink had more than one hundred contacts with the plotters. They had ordered the instructions from Oregon, grown the castor beans, extracted the ricin, and were trying to decide how to use it. IRS agents, U.S. marshals and local sheriff's deputies were suggested targets.

Last August, the FBI arrested Doug Baker and LeRoy Wheeler, who grew the castor beans and whose fingerprints were on the coffee can and rubber gloves. On February 28 of this year, a federal jury convicted them of possessing a biological toxin intended for use as a weapon. Meanwhile the Oregon man who ran "Maynard's Avenging Angel Supply" mail-order business was sent to prison on weapons violations. Had it not been for Doug Baker's indiscretion in pointing a shotgun at his wife, and her delivery of the ricin stash to the police, biological terrorism might have erupted in the United States well ahead of the sarin-gas murders in Tokyo's subway system.

In the wake of the Oklahoma City bombing, Kunstler's CCR struck again. This time it used the Freedom of Information Act to obtain 22 of 199 pages from FBI files on ACT-UP, the militant AIDS activist group. The files showed that, in 1990-91, when the group had scheduled protests at the U.S. Capitol and National Institutes of Health, tipsters told the FBI that some members planned violence to attract media attention. The FBI passed along the tips to relevant law-enforcement agencies and like any good bureaucracy filed them, but did no independent investigation.

But the *Times* and the *Post* once again ran accusatory stories about FBI domestic spying. Steven Michael, chairman of the ACT-UP Washington office, demanded a congressional investigations and told the Post, "They are caught with their hand in the cookie jar. I really genuinely believe that this was politically motivated. Their response is to spy on us. I don't feel safe, I don't feel comfortable. The mere fact that the FBI has a file on my organization frightens me. We have never committed an act of violence. They have no basis to even have page one."

Thus, the campaign to make America safe for terrorists continues. Let the buyer beware. Though all this proved futile as is evident from the 11 September's tragedy.

Bibliography

Anand, V.K., *Terrorism and Security,* New Delhi, Deep and Deep, 1984.

Arora, Subhash Chander, *Strategies to Combat Terrorism: A Study of Punjab,* New Delhi, Har-Anand, 1999.

Bhan, Susheela, *Terrorism: An Annotated Bibliography,* New Delhi, Concept, 1989.

Cameron, Gavin, *Nuclear terrorism: A Threat Assessment for the 21st Century,* London, Macmillan, 1999.

Chalk, Peter, *West European Terrorism and Counter-terrorism: The Evolving Dynamic,* London, Macmillan Press, 1996.

Chakrabarti, Hiren, *Political Protest in Bengal Boycott and Terrorism 1905-1918,* Calcutta, Papyrus, 1992.

Clutterbuck, Richard, *Terrorism and Guerrilla Warfare: Forecasts and Remedies,* London, Routledge, 1990.

Datta, P.S., Insurgency in Northeast: Frontiers, *Frontier,* 29 (6)14, 1996.

Dhokalia, R.P., *Terrorism and International Law,* New Delhi, Indian Society of International Law, 1986.

Global Round Table Conference on International Terrorism. Held to mark the 75th Birth Anniversary late Prime Minister Smt. Indira Gandhi.

Goyal, Archana, *Terrorism: Causes and Consequences,* Bikaner, Institute of Environment, 1990.

Grover, Verinder, *The Story of Punjab Yesterday and Today: Political History and Development with Chronology of Major Political Events,* New Delhi, Deep and Deep, 1995.

Heehs, Peter, *Nationalism, Terrorism, Communalism: Essays in Modern Indian History,* Delhi, Oxford University Press, 1988.

The Hindu, various issues.

The Hindustan Times, various issues.

Indira Deva, M.G., *Terrorist Movement in South India: A Case Study,* Trivandrum, Kerala Historical Society, 1977.

Karism, Afsir, *Counter Terrorism: The Pakistan Factor,* New Delhi, Lancer International, 1991.

Kartha, Tara, *Tools of Terror: Light Weapons and India's Security,* New Delhi, Institute for Defence Studies and Analysis, 1999.

Khurshid, Salman, *Beyond Terrorism: New Hope for Kashmir,* New Delhi, UBSPD, 1994.

Marwah, Ved, *Uncivil Wars: Pathology of Terrorism in India,* New Delhi, Harper Colins, 1995.

Mickolus, Edward F. and Stimmons, Susan L., *Terrorism 1992-1995: A Chronology of Events and Selectively Annotated Bibliography,* Connecticut, London Praeger, 1997.

Mohindra, S., *Terrorist Games Nations Play,* New Delhi, Lancer 1993.

Nandi, Ashish. *The Discrest Charms of Indian Terrorism,* Jr. of Commonwealth and Comparative Politics, 1990.

O'Kane, Rosemary H.T., *Terror, Force and States: The Path for Modernity,* Cheltenham, Edward Elger, 1996.

Omprakash, S., *Terrorism in India,* New Delhi, Ess Ess Pub., 1997.

Paletz, David L. and Schmid Alex P., *Terrorism and the Media,* London, Sage 1993.

Puri, Balraj, *"Jammu Side of Pir Panchal a flame" Mainstream,* 36(26), 1998.

Puri, Harish K. and others, *Terrorism in Punjab: Understanding Grassroots Reality,* New Delhi, Har-Anand, 1999.

Rao, N.P., *Terrorism, Violence and Human Destruction: Causes, Effect and Control Measures.* New Delhi, Anmol, 1992.

Saha. B.P., *Trans-border Terrorism: Internationalization of Kashmir Tangle,* New Delhi, Har-Anand, 1996.

Sahai, Shsi B., *South Asia: From Freedom to Terrorism,* New Delhi, Gyan, 1998.

Sarkar, Bhaskar, *Tackling Insurgency and Terrorism: Blueprint for Action,* New Delhi, Vision Books, 1998.

Shaleshwar Nath, *Terrorism in India,* New Delhi, Nations, 1980.

Sonal Ashish, *Terrorism and Insurgency in India: A Study of Human Element,* New Delhi, Lancer Pubs, 1994.

Subha Rao, S., *Terrorism and Crimes in India,* Bangalore, Gangaram Pub., 1993.

Sehga, B.P. Singh, *Global Terrorism: Socio-political and Legal Dimensions,* New Delhi, Deep and Deep, 1995.

Ray, Ajin, *Is Indian Politically Polluted?: Geo-social Protests and Challenges,* Allahabad, Horizon, 1998.

Taylor, Peter, *States of Terror: Democracy and Political Violence,* London, BBC Books, 1993.

Thomas, K.V. *Human Rights, Terrorism and Policing in India,* New Delhi, Indian Social Institute, 1999.

Vijay Karan, *War by Stealth: Terrorism in India,* New Delhi, Viking, 1997.

Index

□□□